Barcelona, the Left and the Independence Movement in Catalonia

Created by social movement activists and left-wing parties during years of austerity, Barcelona en Comú, or the Comuns (as they are known in Catalan), won control of the city council of Barcelona in May 2015. The ensuing municipal government gave the city its first ever female mayor in the form of former housing rights campaigner, Ada Colau. The Comuns' administration proceeded to undertake ambitious initiatives, attempting to regenerate democracy by changing the relationship between municipal authority and citizens, addressing social inequality issues and seeking to curb the hitherto unbridled tourist expansion in the name of improving the environment for those who live in the Catalan capital.

Barcelona, the Left and the Independence Movement in Catalonia examines the extent to which the political project of the Comuns has brought radical change in Barcelona, where it has faced opposition from revolutionary anti-capitalists, traditional Catalan nationalists and *independentistas*, as well as conservative political and economic forces. It also considers the Comuns' relationship to Podemos and their prospects of growing beyond the city, in the metropolitan area of Barcelona and across Catalonia.

Richard Gillespie is Emeritus Professor of Politics at the University of Liverpool. Before being appointed to the Chair in Politics at the University of Liverpool in 2000, he held posts at the universities of Newcastle, Portsmouth, Warwick and Oxford. His ongoing research interests centre around movements seeking national independence for non-sovereign regions within EU member states, particularly Catalonia.

T0352795

Europa Country Perspectives

The *Europa Country Perspectives* series, from Routledge, examines a wide range of contemporary political, economic, developmental and social issues from areas around the world. Complementing the *Europa Regional Surveys of the World series, Europa Country Perspectives* is a valuable resource for academics, students, researchers, policymakers, business people and anyone with an interest in current world affairs.

While the *Europa World Year Book* and its associated Regional Surveys inform on and analyse contemporary economic, political and social developments at the national and regional level, Country Perspectives provide in-depth, country-specific volumes written or edited by specialists in their field, delving into a country's particular situation. Volumes in the series are not constrained by any particular template, but may explore a country's recent political, economic, international relations, social, defence, or other issues in order to increase understanding.

Russian Nationalism and Ethnic Violence: Symbolic Violence, Lynching, Pogrom, and Massacre
Richard Arnold

Beyond the Drug War in Mexico: Human rights, the public sphere and justice
Wil G. Pansters, Benjamin T. Smith, Peter Watt

Greece in the 21st Century: The Politics and Economics of a Crisis
Edited by Constantine Dimoulas and Vassilis K. Fouskas

The Basque Contention: Ethnicity, Politics, Violence
Ludger Mees

Barcelona, the Left and the Independence Movement in Catalonia
Richard Gillespie

For more information about this series, please visit: www.routledge.com/Europa-Country-Perspectives/book-series/ECP

Barcelona, the Left and the Independence Movement in Catalonia

Richard Gillespie

Routledge
Taylor & Francis Group

LONDON AND NEW YORK

First published 2020
by Routledge
2 Park Square, Milton Park, Abingdon, Oxon OX14 4RN

and by Routledge
52 Vanderbilt Avenue, New York, NY 10017

*Routledge is an imprint of the Taylor & Francis Group, an informa
business*

First issued in paperback 2021

Europa Commissioning Editor: Cathy Hartley

Editorial Assistant: Lucy Pritchard

British Library Cataloguing in Publication Data
A catalogue record for this book is available from the British
Library

Library of Congress Cataloging-in-Publication Data
Names: Gillespie, Richard, 1952- author.
Title: Barcelona, the left and the independence movement in
  Catalonia / Richard Gillespie.
Description: Abingdon, Oxon ; New York, NY : Routledge, 2020. |
  Series: Europa country perspectives | Includes bibliographical
  references and index.
Identifiers: LCCN 2019031119 (print) | LCCN 2019031120 (ebook)
  | ISBN 9781857439625 (hardback) | ISBN 9781351046879
  (ebook)
Subjects: LCSH: Barcelona En Comú (Political organization) |
  Municipal government–Spain–Barcelona. | Barcelona (Spain)–
  Politics and government–21st century. | Catalonia (Spain)–
  History–Autonomy and independence movements.
Classification: LCC JS6335.B3 G45 2020 (print) | LCC JS6335.B3
  (ebook) | DDC 946.7/2084–dc23
LC record available at https://lccn.loc.gov/2019031119
LC ebook record available at https://lccn.loc.gov/2019031120

ISBN: 978-1-85743-962-5 (hbk)
ISBN: 978-1-03-208669-9 (pbk)
ISBN: 978-1-351-04687-9 (ebk)

Typeset in Times New Roman
by Taylor & Francis Books

Contents

Tables

Acknowledgements

In terms of the Catalan context, this book has some foundations in an earlier project on pro-sovereignty politics, but the more focused research has been undertaken since the radical municipalist platform Barcelona en Comú was elected in 2015. While newspapers (including *El País, El Periódico, La Vanguardia, Ara* and *Público*) have been used to track the development of the subject chronologically, it has been interviews with political leaders, activists and some fellow researchers that have contributed to the book's main insights, and it is to them that I am most deeply indebted.

For support and encouragement, I wish also to thank José Magone, Keith Salmon, Paul Kennedy, Esther Barbé, Oriol Bartomeus, Mònica Hernàndez, Caroline Gray, and especially the Europa commissioning editor, Cathy Hartley. Finally, my thanks go to my wife María Elena who accompanied me on all the research visits to Barcelona and provided invaluable support throughout, not least in relation to interview organization and logistics.

Richard Gillespie,
Chester, July 2019

Abbreviations

AMB	Àrea Metropolitana de Barcelona (Metropolitan Area of Barcelona)
AMI	Associació de Municipis per la Independència (Association of pro-Independence Municipalities)
ANC	Assemblea Nacional Catalana (Catalan National Assembly)
BCN Canvi	Barcelona pel Canvi (Barcelona for Change)
BComú	Barcelona en Comú (Barcelona in Common)
CatComú	Catalunya en Comú (Catalonia in Common)
CatComú-Podem	Catalunya en Comú-Podem (Catalonia in Common We Can)
CDC	Convergència Democràtica de Catalunya (Democratic Convergence of Catalonia)
CIE	centro de internamiento de extranjeros (foreigner internment centre)
CiU	Convergència i Unió (Convergence and Unity)
CpC	Ciutadans pel Canvi (Citizens for Change)
Cs	Ciudadanos (Citizens)
CSQP	Catalunya Sí que es Pot (Catalonia Yes We Can)
CUP	Candidatura d'Unitat Popular (Popular Unity Candidature)
DESC	Drets Econòmics, Socials i Culturals (Observatory on Economic, Social and Cultural Rights)
DiEM25	Democracy in Europe Movement 2025
ECP	En Comú Podem (In Common We Can)
EP	European Parliament
ERC	Esquerra Republicana de Catalunya (Republican Left of Catalonia)
EU	European Union

EUiA	Esquerra Unida i Alternativa (United Left and Alternative)
FAVB	Federació d'Associacions de Veïns i Veïnes de Barcelona (Federation of Barcelona Residents Associations)
IC	Iniciativa per Catalunya (Initiative for Catalonia)
ICV	Iniciativa per Catalunya Verds (Initiative for Catalonia Greens)
IGOP	Institut de Govern i Polítiques Públiques (Institute of Government and Public Policy, Autonomous University of Barcelona)
IU	Izquierda Unida (United Left)
JxCat	Junts per Catalunya (Together for Catalonia)
JxSí	Junts pel Sí (Together for the Yes)
MES	Moviment d'Esquerres (Left Movement)
PAD	Programes d'Actuació dels Distrites (Programmes for District Action)
PAH	Plataforma de Afectados por la Hipoteca (Platform for Mortgage Victims)
PAM	Programa d'Actuació Municipal (Programme for Municipal Action)
PDeCAT	Partit Demòcrata Europeu Català (Catalan European Democratic Party)
PEUAT	Plan Especial Urbanístico de Alojamiento (Special Urban Accommodation Plan)
PP	Partido Popular (People's Party)
PSC	Partit dels Socialistes de Catalunya (Socialist Party of Catalonia)
PSOE	Partido Socialista Obrero Español (Spanish Socialist Workers' Party)
PSUC	Partit Socialista Unificat de Catalunya (Unified Socialist Party of Catalonia)
REC	citizens economic resource
UCLG	United Cities and Local Governments
UDC	Unió Democràtica de Catalunya (Democratic Union of Catalonia)
UDI	unilateral declaration of independence
UP	Unidos Podemos (United We Can); renamed Unidas Podemos, 2019

1   Introduction

Created by social movement activists and left-wing parties during years of austerity, *Barcelona en Comú* (BComú) won control of the city council of Barcelona in May 2015. The ensuing municipal government gave the city its first-ever female mayor in the form of former housing rights campaigner, Ada Colau. With the dubious distinction of commanding the fewest council seats ever in Barcelona's history, her administration proceeded to govern through ad hoc support from other parties and, for a while, a coalition with the Partit dels Socialistes de Catalunya (PSC), affiliated to the Partido Socialista Obrero Español (PSOE). Despite its minority status, the administration of the Comuns (as they are known in Catalan) proceeded to undertake ambitious initiatives, attempting to regenerate democracy by changing the relationship between municipal authority and citizens, addressing social inequality issues and seeking to curb the hitherto unbridled tourist expansion in the name of improving the environment for those who live in the Catalan capital.

While associated with the Spanish left-wing party Podemos, created in 2014, BComú has a dynamic and a culture of its own. In the Spanish Parliament, the Comuns are in the same parliamentary group as Podemos, and, in Barcelona the latter's Catalan section, Podem, forms part of the 'confluence' of forces constituting BComú. Yet disagreements emerged with Podem as the Comuns proceeded to construct a new Catalan party, *Catalunya en Comú* (CatComú). When this process bore fruit in 2017, Podem stayed out, although individual Podemos supporters became involved in the new project.

Though CatComú had a disappointing electoral baptism in the Catalan elections of 2017, both it and especially BComú have become significant players in multiple, simultaneously unfolding contests: over left-right policy options in Catalonia, Spain and beyond, but also about the territorial distribution of power, with the Comuns being the only force that straddles the Catalan divide over the question of independence. They assert the right of Catalans to decide the future status of Catalonia vis-à-vis Spain autonomously, but mostly their members wish to avoid separation. In the eyes of many Catalan *independentistas*, they form part of the problem of Spanish dominance, while in the minds of many unionists they have been guilty of collaborating with the independence forces.

At the Spanish level, the Comuns are one of several relatively new parties and electoral platforms that have helped undermine the dominance of the parties that have governed since 1982, namely, the centre-left PSOE and the right-wing Partido Popular (PP). They form part of a trend in some European countries of 'alternative left' initiatives being undertaken following the disappearance of mass communist parties and the difficulties experienced by social democratic parties in dealing with capitalism in the age of globalization. Like Podemos, the Comuns have been allies especially of Syriza in Greece. Ada Colau herself has been a promoter of the Democracy in Europe Movement (DiEM25), associated with former Greek finance minister Yannis Varoufakis.

This book examines the extent to which the political project of the Comuns has brought radical change in Barcelona, where BComú has faced opposition from revolutionary anti-capitalists, traditional Catalan nationalists and *independentistas*, as well as conservative political and economic forces. It also considers the prospects of the Comuns growing beyond the city, in the metropolitan area of Barcelona, across Catalonia and at the Spanish level, for while perceiving the city as the fundamental point of departure for democracy-enhancing efforts, they recognize that their project cannot be realized entirely through municipal efforts.

A key concern of this book is to bring out what is novel, and not so novel, in BComú's political approach, while comparing it with other left-wing forces in Catalonia. The Comuns, like Podemos, are descendants of the *indignado* movement that rose up across Spain in 2011, denouncing the governing 'caste' formed by the two main parties, the corruption pervading political life, the anti-social aspects of globalization and the austere economic policies. In Barcelona, they have attempted to go beyond protest and, while criticizing the distance between elites and citizens associated with representative democracy, they set out to develop political action from the bottom up, with a view to the further empowerment of citizens. Equally novel has been their idea of developing a 'confluence' of left-wing and progressive forces whose politics are shaped less by ideology than by concrete inputs from the grass roots of society, in contrast to old-style attempts to strengthen the left by means of elite pacts negotiated by party leaders.

The structure of the book

This book critically assesses the extent of radical innovation by the Comuns in terms of their ideas, policies, organizational approach and political strategy, considering what has been achieved thus far in terms of confluence on the left and a more participative democracy. The first substantive chapter focuses on the context in which the Comuns emerged as a political force (Chapter 2). This is discussed in at various levels – global, Spanish, Catalan and local – all of which have seen developments influencing their political genesis. Here, one finds a particularly interesting interaction between the local and the global, with the Comuns emerging as part of the anti-globalization movement yet arising out of locally-focused social movements and proceeding to make the city of Barcelona a point of reference for radical municipalist movements worldwide (Chapter 2).

Following this, in Chapter 3, the book examines the rise of Barcelona en Comú: how rethinking within alternative left parties and among social movement activists led to its creation in 2014 and its electoral triumph just a year later; the process whereby a largely successful process of confluence took place in the Catalan capital; and the way in which the new organization set out to renew traditional left-wing thinking by drawing upon recent debates about the concept of 'commons' (Chapter 3).

Thereafter, the focus shifts to BComú in office between 2015 and 2019. Chapter 4 focuses on the difficulties of minority government, made worse by divisions between left-leaning parties as the Catalan independence process unfolded; Chapter 5 examines the Colau administration's efforts to extend public participation and introduce transformative policies in a number of key policy areas, among others, those relating to social inequality, the local economy, the environment and gender issues.

Chapter 6 is devoted to the Comuns' efforts to graduate to intervention at the Catalan level through CatComú. This raises questions about the possibility of emulating the politically successful Barcelona model at higher political levels. It is argued that the tasks of developing a solid, sustainable citizen base here have taken second place to the desire to make an immediate electoral impact and have been hampered by the sheer number of elections in Catalonia since 2015. Moreover, the Comuns have been buffeted by strong pressures to take sides in the polarized contest over independence: the prime focus of mass mobilization and civil society political action during the 2010s. In these circumstances, CatComú's attempt to develop as a confluence of forces has been less successful than that of BComú. The frustration this has brought was leading to the open expression of internal political differences among the Comuns by the time that multiple elections (general, municipal and European) were held during the first half of 2019 (Chapter 7). These elections provided a basis for gauging public responses to the Comuns' performance in political life thus far and their potential to achieve change and exert further influence in the future. At the municipal level, many reforms were still unfolding and required a further period of office if they were to become consolidated. What happened in these elections in Barcelona and beyond was to be of huge interest, not only to antagonists in the independence and left-right contests within Spain, but also to people on different sides of the globalization debate in Europe and the Americas.

2 Outlining the context

The origins of Barcelona en Comú are to be found in the context of widespread social, economic and political dissatisfaction with the established order, whose most graphic expression was the widespread protest movement of the *indignados* ('outraged ones') that swept Spain in May 2011, becoming known as the 15-M movement. This experience eventually led radicals to combine in new ways with a view to channelling public protest into the construction of a radical political movement, amid signs that this had some chance of municipal electoral success at a time of growing fragmentation in the party system both across Spain and within Catalonia. The social context was marked by the austerity policies subscribed to by both the PP (Partido Popular, People's Party) and the PSOE (Partido Socialista Obrero Español, Spanish Socialist Workers' Party) by 2010, undertaken in response to the global financial and economic crisis, compounded by the national collapse of the Spanish construction industry and property market. It was shaped too by longer-term aspects of globalization such as the growth of mass tourism from abroad and its ecological impact on the city of Barcelona.

Economic conditions and austerity politics prompted a rise in social movement activity right across Spain, but nowhere was this as vigorous as in Barcelona, with its long history of radical protest and cultural creativity. Since the global financial crisis of 2008, social inequalities had worsened throughout Spain, but in Barcelona and Catalonia the discontent was overlain also with a growing sense of injustice over territorially-configured disparities. While Barcelona experienced a particularly acute economic crisis, many Catalans began to express grievances over the amount they were contributing to poorer regions of Spain through inter-regional financial transfer mechanisms and about the neglect of their community by central government, which they saw reflected in a deteriorating regional infrastructure – especially the road and rail networks.

Equally, the rise of an 'alternative left' must be viewed against the decline of traditional left parties, the crisis of the party system that had existed since the Spanish transition to democracy in the 1970s and popular disillusionment with representative democracy, encapsulated in the *indignado* protest slogan, 'they don't represent us'. BComú came into being at a time when many Catalans were embracing pro-independence political options and thus challenging the Spanish political system in other ways, but there existed a political window of opportunity for a municipally-based left-wing resurgence in Catalonia too, not least because the leading party within the independence movement up to 2015 was a nationalist entity that was right of centre. Convergència Democràtica de Catalunya (CDC), refounded in 2016 as the Partit Demòcrata Europeu Català (PDeCAT), had become neo-liberal in economic outlook since the 1990s under the successive leaderships of Jordi Pujol and Artur Mas. It was the dominant partner of the Unió Democràtica de Catalunya (UDC) in the Convergència i Unió (CiU) party federation, which had pursued austerity policies after being returned to office in Catalonia in 2010 and had collaborated with the PP at various levels of government until 2012.

There is also an international context here of the rise of city politics, seen in many metropolitan centres of the world, yet of singular significance in the case of Barcelona. Traditional Catalan nationalism had worked to amass as much power as possible in the regional government, the *Generalitat*, exploiting the fact that devolution in Spain has been essentially regional in direction. Eventually this helped shape the character of the Catalan sovereignty challenge of 2017, by which time many Catalans perceived their nation to be locked in a zero-sum game with the Spanish state, centred in Madrid. However, territorial dimensions to political competition have been present too *within* Catalonia, with centre-right nationalists seeing Barcelona and its city hall (*Ajuntament*) as a potential political rival to the *Generalitat*. While presiding over the latter between 1980 and 2003, Pujol successfully resisted the ambitions of Pasqual Maragall, the Socialist mayor from 1982 to 1997, to gain more municipal autonomy and establish a stronger metropolitan governance body based on democratic representation. In response to Maragall's efforts to strengthen the Corporación Metropolitana de Barcelona – a developmentalist institution created in 1974 with a bigger remit than today's Área Metropolitana de Barcelona (AMB) – Pujol made use of CiU's control of the provincial government of Barcelona to abolish the corporation in 1987.

The global dimension

Although local in its initial electoral focus, Barcelona en Comú has been characterized by a global outlook and awareness since its origins. It has identified itself with the transnational anti-globalization movement. The Comuns perceived the politics of austerity implemented by the traditional parties prior to 2018 as reflecting neo-liberal trends across western countries and within international institutions, resulting in a serious erosion of democracy and accountability as well as increased inequality. However, BComú has been marked by eclecticism and cannot be defined purely in terms of an anti-globalization characterization. Although effectively a party, it describes itself more as a common 'space' for political activism and is politically broad enough to share some common ground with social democrats as well as involve elements descending from the old Catalan Communist Party, the Partit Socialista Unificat de Catalunya (PSUC). There is also the Comuns' positive evaluation of some aspects of globalization, especially the opportunities afforded by new digital communications media to promote political messages and facilitate the building of networks of citizens and of cities grappling with common challenges. The appeal of globalization, albeit strongly qualified in the case of the Comuns, is understandable in a country that had experienced decades of international isolation under Franco (González-Enríquez, 2017: 17).

To some extent, too, BComú has associated itself with the 'new' or 'alternative' left currents seen in other parts of Europe, including France and Germany, since the 1960s, and with more recent radical movements in Latin America, notably the Zapatistas in Mexico. The Zapatista uprising of 1994, involving an assertion of local autonomy and self-government, was hailed by the *indignados* in Spain as the first revolt against the 'New World Order' defined by neo-liberalism (Antentas and Vivas, 2011: 15; Observatorio Metropolitano, 2014: 47–71). Contemporaneously, like Podemos, and especially before the Tsipras government acquiesced to EU demands in 2015, the Comuns demonstrated a special affinity with Syriza, formed through a realignment of left-wing forces opposed to neo-liberal orthodoxy in Greece.

Barcelona en Comú thus sees itself as part of various international movements and has not focused its activity on the big anti-globalization protests of recent years so much as fight back municipally against the impact of globally-driven policies that have eroded the living standards and rights of most sections of society, while also undermining local government. Its appearance as a political force reflected the emergence of new social, cultural and political loyalties and renewed public interest in civic engagement resulting from need, as people reacted to the prevalence of neo-liberal ideas over traditional social democratic models (Eizaguirre, Pradel-Miquel and García, 2017: 425–427). In response to these trends, BComú identifies with traditions of municipalism on a global scale, but with special reference to Europe and the Americas (Shea Baird, 2017) and also across Spain where it sees a history marked by phases of local assertiveness on the part of civil society, alternating with periods of institutionalization when interaction between local government and the grassroots has been more limited. The election of 'councils for change' in several major Spanish cities in May 2015 promised to make political life revolve more around the citizenry and seemed to vindicate the decision taken by social movement activists to join with alternative left parties in the name of 'reclaiming the city' through contesting these elections with a firm determination to triumph and introduce transformative change.

The Spanish context

This contextual discussion invites consideration of the extent to which Barcelona en Comú should be conceived as a 'Spanish' or even *españolista* (Spanish unionist) phenomenon, as some Catalan pro-independence parties claim it to be. Certainly, the Comuns place themselves partly in the historical traditions of Spanish republicanism and municipalism going back to the nineteenth century, whose progressive promise bore fruit politically following phases of centralist dictatorship – most recently after Franco's demise in 1975. During the ensuing transition to democracy, Spain experienced several years of democratic municipal revival accompanied by a rise in social and political activism and the growth of local neighbourhood associations. The city of Barcelona had 70,000 residents' association members by 1978 (Balfour, 1989: 195). However, the victory of the left in Spain's municipal elections in 1979, the gradual establishment of a regional tier of government across Spain and the electoral victory of the PSOE under Felipe González in 1982 led many activists to move on from associational involvement into governmental, administrative or advisory roles, causing civil society organizations to decline as the new democracy became institutionalized.

The new Spanish model of democracy involved various mechanisms to consolidate the position of a reduced number of parties (essentially two), to the point that it was referred to by some critics as a 'party state'. Though the dominance of these parties (and of leadership elites within them) brought problems, such as corruption and the under-representation of political minorities, Spain experienced periods of impressive economic growth and rising living standards, assisted by entry to the EU in 1986; thus overall there was extensive public satisfaction with what was seen to be a 'consolidated democracy'. Only after the global financial crisis had brought misery to the construction industry and property market did the collapse of growth and the rise of unemployment – reaching 26 per cent of the economically active population (twice as high among young people) – generate a widespread public sense of systemic failure, particularly once the PSOE, as well as the PP, had decided that there was no alternative to severe austerity as the means of addressing major sovereign debt and budget deficit crises and eventually emerging from the great recession.

Social movement activism revived in the early years of this recession as people began to see politicians collectively and their political parties as part of the problem, incapable of providing solutions. Victims of the recession looked partly to family solidarity to mitigate the hardship, yet there was increased interest too in joining forces with others in a similar condition, to protest, lobby and find practical solutions. The most salient organization was the Platform for Mortgage Victims (PAH, Plataforma de Afectados por la Hipoteca), bringing together people whose mortgages were foreclosed in response to repayment difficulties. Organized democratically, structured horizontally rather than hierarchically and eliciting considerable neighbourhood solidarity, it staged demonstrations and occupations to put pressure on banks to negotiate acceptable alternatives to simply repossessing homes, and also helped victims find places to live. Created in Barcelona in 2009, the PAH gradually spread to the rest of Spain. It successfully organized an appeal to the European Court of Justice, which in March 2013 ruled that Spain's rigid approach to home repossessions did not comply with the protection of the consumer directive of 1993. The ruling affected some 250,000 mortgage repossessions that had taken place in 2008–2012, allowing victims to sue for compensation. Thereafter, accusations of abusive behaviour by banks sometimes led judges to suspend repossession proceedings (Magone, 2018: 234). The PAH became a key example of how direct action, combined with litigation, not only can highlight malpractices but also can bring practical solutions to the problems experienced by groups of disadvantaged people.

The PAH was centrally involved in the 15-M movement of 2011, which saw lengthy occupations of central public spaces in big cities not only to protest but also to hold workshops and assemblies to discuss political alternatives based on 'real' democracy. *Indignado* demands included electoral reform (to strengthen proportional representation and develop new channels for citizen participation), total political transparency (to combat corruption), an effective separation of powers and the creation of citizens' control mechanisms, designed to ensure political responsibility and representativeness (Taibo et al., 2011: 92).

As spokesperson for the PAH, Ada Colau became a high-profile national figure, known especially for her speech in the Spanish Parliament in February 2013, when she went to present a popular legislative initiative based on 1.4 million signatures collected by the PAH, calling for major changes in mortgage arrangements and greater social housing provision (Colau and Alemany, 2013; De Weert and García, 2015). In Spain, private home ownership had been promoted by governments since the 1950s and accounted for 87 per cent of the housing market by 2007, while the availability of rented property was well below the EU average and the public rented sector was just 1 per cent. Thus, in the aftermath of the financial crisis, mortgage problems featured prominently as a source of social discontent, which soon extended to the rented sector as well, as those losing their own homes faced new difficulties, especially following government measures to facilitate the eviction of tenants for failing to pay rent and a liberalization of controls over rent levels in 2011–2012 (Colau and Alemany, 2012: 31–49).

While central government focused on financial and economic priorities, its failure to address the social crisis prompted a rise in civil society efforts to tackle problems directly and seek a measure of local control. A broader and longer-term context was provided by the way that the power of financial markets and the neo-liberal political dominance had been tending to undermine local representative democracy. Cities were now being seen increasingly by their councils as a place to do business and were trying to compete with one other; citizens thus saw their public space commercialized and foreign investment courted, raising the spectre in some places of their being transformed into theme parks for tourists (Garcia, 2017).

An increasing subordination of political institutions to entrepreneurs (especially property magnates in the case of Barcelona) was exacerbated once the period of austerity had arrived. Despite the post-Franco democratization, municipal government in Spain had remained constrained by a relatively weak financial base compared with northern Europe, making a large proportion of income reliant on local property development; and it now saw this drop dramatically because of the crisis in the construction sector. Making matters worse, the PP under Rajoy used the economic crisis as an opportunity to centralize financial powers, impose disproportionate spending cuts at the regional and local levels and reduce the role of municipal government (especially in small localities) through the Law of Rationalization and Sustainability of Local Administrations of 2013, citing as pretexts both international and EU pressure on Spain to reduce its budget deficit drastically and a pressing need to put an end to administrative duplication (Observatorio Metropolitano, 2014, 81–98; Muro, 2015).

Catalan and local contexts

The Catalan context is hugely important for this study, for several reasons: Barcelona's status as a regional capital, the way in which 'autonomous communities' such as Catalonia constrain, compete and cooperate with municipal authorities, and because the parties possessing an institutional presence in the city also aspire to control the *Generalitat*, through winning elections to the Catalan *Parlament*. The province of Barcelona elects 85 of the 135 seats in the parliament, compared with Tarragona 18, Girona 17 and Lleida 15. Each level of government has a distinct political biosphere, not least because the calendars for elections to regional and municipal governance structures differ. Yet Barcelona needs to respond to the wider dynamics of Catalan politics and it projects its own demands and ambitions towards the Catalan level, which has responsibility for important areas of policy, such as education, healthcare, regional development and policing. In recent years, the issue of Catalan independence has become *the* most challenging one, demanding statements of position and practical responses from the city authorities, notwithstanding their specific concerns with municipal issues. It has been challenging because support for independence has grown in Barcelona itself, as shown by the gains made by the nationalist, social democratic Esquerra Republicana de Catalunya (ERC) and the anti-capitalist Candidatura d'Unitat Popular (CUP) in 2015.

Traditionally, independence sentiments have been much higher in the interior of Catalonia, while the capital and metropolitan area – historically more affected by economic development and migration from other parts of Spain and today possessing a more cosmopolitan population – have mostly advocated a continuing relationship with Madrid. The unprecedented victory of CiU in 2011, whereby Xavier Trias became mayor of Barcelona, demonstrated not only the erosion of support for the established forces of the left after eight years in the government of Catalonia and three decades of municipal dominance, but also the availability of support in the capital for more unequivocally Catalanist[1] political alternatives, free of affiliations to Spanish parties. It led to four years of apparent harmony over the independence issue between the regional and city authorities, as Trias himself refrained from expressing his long-standing moderately autonomist views, by now at odds with the *independentista* discourse embraced by his party, CDC, following a process of radicalization of its territorial postulates (Gillespie, 2017a). After 2015, however, with the election of the Comuns in the city and their eventual coalition with the PSC, that tension became more acute as the agendas of the *Generalitat* and the *Ajuntament*, facing each other across the Plaça de Sant Jaume, diverged.

It is necessary to take a longer view of the relationship between Catalonia and Barcelona for, although their party systems have seen particularly dramatic changes over the last decade (Culla, 2017), there were signs of tension between Catalan and municipal ambitions, interwoven with different political agendas, much earlier. From the end of the Spanish transition of the late 1970s, the pattern that long characterized Catalonian politics was regional government by CiU, in government from 1980 to 2003 and again from 2010 to 2015 (at times with support from ERC), and left-wing dominance of the city and metropolitan area of Barcelona, where leadership up to 2011 came primarily from the PSC, often governing locally in coalitions with smaller left-wing partners. Socialist allies included the PSUC, its descendant Iniciativa per Catalunya (IC), which went on to ally with the Greens to become the eco-socialist Iniciativa per Catalunya Verds, ICV, and Esquerra Unida i Alternativa (EUiA), another left-wing alliance, including Communist and post-Communist elements but with a stronger Spanish orientation as part of the state-wide Izquierda Unida (IU).

The Spanish devolution model, the political agenda of CiU and the latter's ability to extract concessions from Madrid in return for supporting PSOE and PP minority governments in Madrid all contrived to centralize the Catalan power structure primarily at the regional level, where the powers of the Generalitat grew periodically over the years. During his long term as president of the Catalan government, Jordi Pujol resisted proposals to enhance the political authority of Barcelona and acted to frustrate the possibility of the city being able to acquire metropolitan hegemony, although after abolishing the Corporación Metropolitana, a pragmatic assessment of mutual benefit was seen in the Generalitat's collaboration with the city council over Barcelona's hosting of the Olympic Games in 1992. Within the city, meanwhile, left-wing administrations were headed for much of this period by Pasqual Maragall of the PSC. He saw an increase in municipal power as a means to enhance democracy and work for a more equitable distribution of wealth, while viewing cities as the prime loci of connectivity with other parts of Spain, Europe and the world. Although there had been a much earlier campaign by José María de Porcioles (mayor, 1957–1973) to enhance the powers of the city, this had been driven by the desire to promote business opportunities. Maragall was the first mayor of Barcelona to address urban development in a comprehensive way, pursue a more socially inclusive development strategy and introduce elements of citizen participation in governance. Although defeated in the battle over the Corporación Metropolitana, as president of the Generalitat in 2003–2006, he went on to lay the basis for the establishment of the AMB (finally created under his successor, José Montilla, in 2011), while undertaking limited initiatives in relation to decentralization and devolution to the municipal level (Pradel-Miquel, 2016).

Metropolitan outreach from Barcelona was of growing relevance owing to changes in demographic patterns and the local economy. By the 1960s, one could no longer speak distinctly of city and metropolitan area since they had become 'joined in one massive urban sprawl' and, through the displacement of industry from centre to periphery, over half the working class were now living in the 'area' (Balfour, 1989: 43). The city's population reached a peak of 1.9 million in 1979 within a metropolitan area of some 3 million, after which it fell, only to stabilize at around 1.6 million thanks to an increase in foreign residents from the 1990s (Tomàs Fornés, 2017: 42). By then, the city had become dominated by the service sector and, in the 1990s, tourism really took off, making Barcelona a phenomenon of global attraction.

Metropolitan expansion generated a functionalist need for integrated services in areas such as transport, water, waste management and energy, and hence for metropolitan-level decision-making. So far, there has been only administrative rationalization, initially through the Metropolitan Corporation, based on 27 municipalities, and more recently through the AMB, based on 36, but still only covering the core of the real metropolitan region (ibid.: 38). In terms of representation, the AMB was designed in such a way as to avoid dominance by the city of Barcelona. Although Barcelona's mayor presides over the metropolitan entity, the city has only 25 of the 90 seats on the governing body, despite having half the population of the administered area of 3.2 million. Moreover, a balance is ensured by means of a deputy president (and effective coordinator of the AMB) being chosen from among the other mayors. When Colau was elected to preside over the area in 2015, the deputy was Antonio Balmón, the PSC mayor of Cornellà de Llobregat. Crucially it is still the town halls in each municipality that decide where investments are to be made. The idea of moving to a directly elected metropolitan president, potentially in a region incorporating 5 million Catalans, has always been strongly resisted by Socialist (and other) mayors of the AMB, and in view of their opposition, would only be mooted tentatively by Colau over the next four years.

Pasqual Maragall broke with traditional party-dominated approaches to political activity by seeking to involve the talent and expertise to be found in civil society, especially among middle-class professionals and intellectuals. While presiding over the PSC in 2000–2007, and promoting asymmetrical federalism as a model for Spain, a new autonomy statute for Catalonia and social improvements, he faced much opposition from the so-called 'captains' in the party organization who had gradually displaced Catalanist intellectuals from the PSC leadership from 1994 onwards (Ernest Maragall interview, 10 February 2014). His political career was cut short by their opposition to his re-election in 2006, after which Alzheimer's disease forced his premature retirement from political life.

Maragall had asserted a degree of autonomy with respect to the PSC by establishing his own civil society platform, Citizens for Change (CpC), in 1998 and he headed a PSC-CpC alliance in the Catalan elections of 1999 and 2003. This formula brought the Socialists their highest vote ever in regional elections in the first of these contests, before a drop in the CiU vote and the ending of its collaboration with the PP allowed the Socialists to be elected in the second, by forming a coalition with ERC and ICV-EUiA (known in Spanish as the *Tripartito*). The eventual replacement of Maragall by Montilla confirmed the impression in Catalonia of the PSC as a franchise party, subordinate to the discipline of the PSOE, although at moments in its history it has defended its organizational autonomy and pressed its federalist advocacy vis-à-vis the Spanish party (Roller and Van Houten, 2003).

The Tripartito also owed its origins to Maragall's championing of a new, enhanced statute of autonomy for Catalonia (to replace that of 1979) at a time when Pujol was still politically constrained by his partnership with the centralist PP and had in any case announced his retirement from public office from 2003. Temporarily, the combined forces of the left were able to seize the Catalanist mantle from CiU and produce the first draft of a new statute, one that would refer to Catalonia as a nation and would make Catalan the main language, no longer simply co-official with Spanish, while also increasing regional powers and seeking a bilaterally negotiated fiscal pact with the central government. The financial objective was to guard against the risk of Catalonia being disadvantaged as a relatively prosperous region in a state committed to inter-regional transfers through its general regional financing system, from which only Euskadi and Navarre (with their own treasuries) had secured exemption.

CiU, however, now led by Artur Mas, was able to extract concessions from the tripartite coalition by exploiting its need for support in the Catalan Parliament in order to achieve the qualified majority required for statute reform. Indeed, CiU tried to outbid ERC through its sovereignty-related demands, taking advantage of the compromises that this party had to make while working with coalition partners that were mindful of the sensibilities of their Spanish counterparts and of the need for the statute, following its approval in Catalonia, to be approved by the Spanish Parliament.

This was the left's first experience of coalition government since the 1930s, and it sorely lacked a culture of coalition. The Tripartito's party components each tended to prevail in the policy sectors for which they had government responsibility, rather than acquiring a sense of collective ownership of a common programme (Jaume Bosch interview, 11 February 2014). Despite now being in opposition in Catalonia, CiU took advantage of the situation to negotiate directly with Socialist prime minister José Luís Rodríguez Zapatero, whose government presided over a dilution of the original draft of the statute, once this had reached the Spanish Parliament. The final text disappointed ERC so much that it opposed it when it was put to Catalans in a referendum in June 2006. It was endorsed by 78 per cent of those voting, on a low turnout of 48.8 per cent. Within the Catalan Parliament, only the PP was entirely opposed to this new statute, but it proceeded to lodge an appeal with the Constitutional Court, for being a constitutional change by the back door. The travails of the statute left the tripartite coalition with a reputation for deep disunity, both between and within its parties, yet it proved able to reassemble itself and return to office, under Montilla, following another Catalan election in November 2006. The Tripartito was finally undermined by the impact of the global financial crisis and further factional schisms, particularly within ERC, which enabled CiU under Mas to return to office in 2010, once more with support initially from the PP. Together the socio-economic hardship experienced during the great recession and the crippling divisions within the coalition left a public impression of failure, with developments during its final years tending to eclipse a record of genuine improvements in the education and healthcare sectors.

By this time, Catalans were increasingly resorting to protest action. The growing independence movement began to acquire public visibility from 2009 by staging a series of unofficial local referendums (*consultas*) on independence in some of the smaller municipalities. Discontent over the relationship with Spain finally became massive following the Constitutional Court ruling on the statute in June 2010, which declared 15 articles unconstitutional, including the definition of Catalonia as a nation and the upgrading of Catalan to the status of main language. The blocking by Spanish actors and institutions of Catalan initiatives to achieve greater political, financial and cultural autonomy, following the raising of hopes of enhancement, thus acted as a catalyst for the spread of pro-independence sentiments. Equally, from 2010, a dialectic of interaction between the Catalan and Spanish governments contributed to radicalization, as relations between them worsened. Catalan support for independence rose from traditional levels of less than 20 per cent to reach 49 per cent in 2013 (Real Instituto Elcano, 2017), and a clear majority of Catalans now backed a referendum on the issue. While dual identity remained a feature of the main sector of public opinion (formed by Catalans describing themselves as 'equally Spanish and Catalan'), the proportion of those feeling predominantly or exclusively Catalan had risen gradually, from 24 per cent in 1979 to more than 40 per cent by the start of the new century (Serrano, 2013: 527–528).

Beyond the immediate drivers of Catalan pro-sovereignty demands, one must see these developments in the context of more gradual processes that have brought changes to the pattern of Catalan preferences. One of these was generational change. Whereas the generation that emerged politically during the 1970s were more persuaded of the need to reach accommodations between major political forces in the interests of stabilizing the new Spanish democracy and facilitating the return of autonomy to Catalonia, those born since the death of Franco have no experience of the repressive past that had left many of their parents inclined towards compromise. Moreover, among the one-third of the population born since the death of Franco, most had been educated in a Catalan education system that, from the 1980s – and by agreement among all the Catalan parties – had decided to make Catalan the basic language used in the schools. While Spanish continued to be the main language used habitually in Catalonia, particularly around Barcelona (Real Instituto Elcano, 2017), the cultural change has been marked, especially among the offspring of Spaniards, who had moved to Catalonia for work reasons: while the older generation tended to continue speaking Spanish and voted for Spanish parties, their sons and daughters proved open to more Catalanist options.

Another process to be borne in mind, given the rise of a narrative of Catalonia being a victim of financial injustice, as encapsulated in the slogan *Espanya ens roba* ('Spain is robbing us'), is the trend whereby in recent decades Catalonia has lost regional pre-eminence as Madrid has advanced, partly through providing the Spanish capital city at a time of internationalization of the economy. Neither this, nor Spain's system of redistributing income from richer to poorer regions, had caused mass political dissent in Catalonia so long as growth remained a reality or economic crises seemed short-lived, but when the global financial crisis arrived, Catalonia experienced growing debt and deficit pressures. Then both the relative neglect of Catalonia in terms of state investment and the fact that it was contributing more in taxation than it was receiving in state expenditure gave fuel to the belief that Catalonia might be better off separate from Spain

(Guibernau, 2014; Boylan, 2015), or at least if it could find some way of reconstituting its relationship with Spain on a federal or confederal basis. This attribution of responsibility for Catalonia's woes to 'Madrid' was questioned by centre-right unionist parties such as the PP and Ciudadanos (Cs), critical of the record of economic management during the long years of CiU governance at regional level.

Socio-economic hardship during the great recession meanwhile gave rise to, or strengthened, social movements, generally led by people with no involvement in institutional political life and indeed often sceptical about conventional politics and parties. They thus based their campaigns on self-help, primarily at the local level, while putting pressure on the political authorities and financial institutions through protests and occupations, many of which – given the breadth and depth of the social crisis – attracted widespread community solidarity beyond the ranks of the movements' activists. According to a study by the Economic and Social Council of Barcelona in 2018, the city witnessed a loss of purchasing power of 6.1 per cent between 2010 and 2016 (compared with 5.4 per cent in Catalonia and 3.9 per cent in Spain), primarily because of higher mortgage and rent costs, affecting among others the middle classes. As a proportion of the population, the middle classes fell from 58.5 to 41.8 per cent between 2007 and 2011 before becoming a majority again in 2017 (*El País*, 9 November 2018, 29 January 2019).

Catalonia had long been one of the regions with the highest indicators of associational life in Spain (Mota and Subirats, 2002: 113–118). Barcelona itself had been the capital of political protest back in the 1970s and was again so now, more than 30 years later. From local origins in Barcelona, the PAH had risen to prominence across Spain during the 15-M mobilizations of 2011. Other influential associations were essentially Catalan in scope. Most prominent among these were Òmnium Cultural, an organization established in the 1960s to revive the Catalan language and culture, as expressed in its slogan 'Language, Culture, Country'. It underwent a revival after 2002 under a younger, more modern leadership, which managed to broaden its appeal sociologically from a traditional base among the elderly, educated middle classes. It committed itself to the goal of independence in 2012, having decided that there was no real possibility of a federal relationship with Spain even becoming a reality. Òmnium collaborated closely with the Assemblea Nacional Catalana (ANC), created in 2011 by activists who wanted to go beyond the one-off efforts around *consultas* by creating a permanent umbrella organization for all pro-independence Catalans (Casals and Garbarró interview, 12 February 2014; Forcadell interview, 26 November 2013 ; Crameri, 2015: 104–120).

The rapid growth of the pro-independence movement was seen from 2011 in huge annual mobilizations on September 11, the day of the *Diada* national festival commemorating the fall of Barcelona during the War of the Spanish Succession in 1714. Initially this found no great response from unionists in Catalonia, but with Madrid showing no readiness to negotiate with the government of Artur Mas, Catalan society eventually became more polarized between pros and antis. However, a more complex map of public preferences underlay this simplification. The prospects of those aiming to establish a Catalan state depended on a broader swathe of Catalanist opinion extending beyond the pro-independence forces themselves to include those who hoped to achieve an enhancement of Catalonia's status via a Spanish constitutional reform, among them people who echoed the demand of the independence movement for a 'right to decide' Catalonia's relationship to Spain through a regional referendum, while opposing separation. The pro-sovereignty (*soberanista*) sector of Catalan society, which now included significant numbers of people whose primary language was Spanish, wanted to see Catalonia's status become differentiated from other Spanish regions, without their community breaking with Spain and risking exclusion from the EU. These people were persuaded of the need for mass mobilization by the intransigence of the central government under Rajoy and of the traditional Spanish parties when faced with successive Catalan governments' requests for a bilateral fiscal pact and authorization of a referendum to enable Catalans to vote on the future relationship of Catalonia to Spain. Significant parts of the PSC subscribed to Catalan sovereignty-based demands and provided the basis for internal currents that in some cases broke away from the mother party over the 'right to decide', while the party vote declined dramatically between 2008 and 2017.

It was against this backcloth that Barcelona en Comú came to be founded, aiming to engage in a new politics, while not eschewing dialogue with those elements of the old left that were reconsidering their approach to political action. Both old and new left elements would be involved in an unfolding process of change in the pattern of political competition in Catalonia, as the question of independence gradually grew in salience.

Note

1 The term 'Catalanist' refers to people and forces that defend and promote the Catalan language and culture, and, when used in a political sense, it also implies a special emphasis on Catalonia as a context for governance, support for Catalan autonomy and at least some emphasis on specifically Catalan

political issues. It thus embraces a wide spectrum of opinion, including advocates of independence, federalism or confederalism who believe that Catalans as a nation have a right to determine their relationship to the Spanish state (rather than sovereignty being vested, as the Constitution stipulates, in the Spanish people as a whole). Of late, the term has been used largely to refer to nationalist parties and sections of the left, although historically it has had conservative political expressions as well (Dowling, 2018: 60). Its application is perhaps most controversial when applied to the Catalan Socialist Party which, through its affiliation to the Spanish party, bears the initials PSC-PSOE and accepts central party discipline for PSC members of the Spanish Parliament, yet, unlike other regional federations of the PSOE, has a separate statute governing its relations with the Spanish party.

3   The making of Barcelona en Comú

Out of the 15 May movement of 2011, little emerged immediately to herald political change. The creative protest movement had been defined by opposition to relentless austerity policies pursued since 2010 and widespread dissatisfaction with a political establishment devoid of alternatives and tainted by corruption scandals, notably the Gürtel case relating to illegal funding of the Partido Popular (PP). According to opinion polls, public dissatisfaction with political life had increased from 13.6 per cent in 2008 to 37.3 per cent by 2013, while specific dissatisfaction with the functioning of democracy had grown from 45.9 per cent to 84.2 per cent (Tugas, 2014: 28). However, the ideas for change emanating from the 15-M were diffuse and impossible to operationalize overnight. Even the 'big idea' of somehow improving or deepening democracy gave rise to different proposals, some of which envisaged the involvement of the more reformist elements of the traditional left while others – looking to the initiation of a new constituent period – did not. There was uncertainty over which, if any, stream of advocacy might prosper and in this situation it was essentially a rejection of existing governments that prevailed in the elections in Barcelona, Catalonia and across Spain. In November 2010, Catalan voters ended seven years of left-wing coalition by giving victory to CiU (Convergència i Unió, Convergence and Unity), led by Artur Mas, who proceeded to form a minority government with support from the PP, and went on to be re-elected two years later. In May 2011, voters in the Catalan capital acted to put an end to 32 years of PSC-led centre-left municipal government, allowing CiU to capture Barcelona for the first time, under veteran politician Xavier Trias. Finally, in the general election the following November, it was Rajoy's PP that won an absolute majority as his party recorded its highest vote to date and the socialist PSOE its lowest since 1977.

At the institutional level, Spain thus saw a shift to the right. Many traditional left-wing voters felt unrepresented or inadequately represented by the leaders of the PSOE and United Left (Izquierda Unida, IU). Yet amid considerable public disorientation and estrangement from the institutions of state, those hard hit by austerity, especially young people and owner-occupiers who had lost their homes and found themselves part of an 'ever more downwardly mobile middle class' (Zechner, 2015), were not reduced to despairing resignation. Rather, growing numbers resorted to direct action. Opposition to the status quo became at least as much focused on social movements as on political parties, the former with narrower but more urgent agendas.

While the Catalan left noted the shift to the right, it was slow to recognize the extent to which this scenario was overlain by a rise in *soberanista* (pro-sovereignty) and *independentista* (pro-independence) sentiment, reflected in the evolving agendas of ERC (Esquerra Republicana de Catalunya, Republican Left of Catalonia) and CiU, slowly increasing support for the CUP (Candidatura d'Unitat Popular, Popular Unity Candidature) and the growth of pro-independence civil society organizations. The Rajoy government's rejection of demands by Mas for a new regional funding model specifically for Catalonia, together with civil society pressures, finally pushed his CDC (Convergència Democràtica de Catalunya, Democratic Convergence of Catalonia) party decisively in the direction of independence politics, which began to dominate the agenda of the Generalitat after the 2012 election, with governmental collaboration commencing between CiU and ERC. It would take another two to three years before the territorial challenge to the status quo itself became complicated by the rise of the alternative left at the municipal level.

The constituent elements of Barcelona en Comú

Reorientation of left-wing parties

The four years stretching from the 15-M to the election of BComú in 2015 saw processes of confluence and alignment between different political groupings and civil society organizations, accompanied by the entry of new actors into political life. From afar, this tended to be interpreted in terms of party political developments, especially the challenge to traditional parties from new ones. The best-known of the new parties internationally was Podemos, which won representation in the European elections of 2014, just a few months after being founded, primarily by left-wing lecturers at the Complutense University of

Madrid. Some, including leader Pablo Iglesias, had previously been active in the Communist Party and the broader United Left, or alternatively in Trotskyist politics, yet all were now proclaiming the advent of a new, more citizen-based politics, premised upon the exhaustion of the post-Franco political system.

Podemos sought to build a socio-political movement based on a confluence of forces that would work on a common project of radical change; it aimed at making an immediate impact in elections, thus enabling the alternative left to go beyond the politics of protest and pursue eventual political hegemony. To some extent, Podemos became a new party of the left, distinguished by its fundamental use of the Internet and new social media to connect political leadership directly with supporters in a non-bureaucratic fashion, especially with young people being drawn into political contestation for the first time. At the same time, it commenced its life with a deliberate populist appeal, under the post-Marxist ideological influence of Ernesto Laclau and Chantal Mouffe. Traditional class-based politics was subsumed in a depiction of social conflict that featured, on one side, a relatively small ruling oligarchy or 'caste' that included not only the socio-economic elites but also the whole Spanish political class established during the post-Franco transition, and, on the other, the mass of ordinary citizens, suffering under a neo-liberal global order.

Podemos found expression in Catalonia as in the rest of Spain, although here it tended to be dominated by the 'anti-capitalist' current influenced by Trotskyism rather than by the post-communist and populist elements. Together with two smaller Spanish parties, Equo, created by Green parties in 2011, and the X Party, advocating citizen-based democracy, Podemos would eventually take part in the creation of BComú. However, the latter was far from synonymous with Podemos. The Comuns' constitutive base was broader, they remained independent of Podemos and had a distinctive vision of how to develop a confluence process. As will be discussed in Chapter 6, the Catalan branch of Podemos would decide not to take part when the confluence approach was attempted at the regional level.

In Catalonia, Podemos has been somewhat handicapped by its associations with Spanish leadership. Mindful of opposition to Catalan self-determination in most other regions of Spain, Podemos at state level was slow to support the territory's 'right to decide'. Even after it did so, many Catalan left-wing and nationalist voters continued to see it as a party 'led from Madrid' by an inner circle around Iglesias, who at times exhibited centralist tendencies in the management of Podemos, contradicting a proclaimed commitment to subsidiarity in relation to decision-making. When the party entered the Spanish political landscape by winning 8 per cent of the vote in the European elections of 2014, it managed only 4.6 per cent in Catalonia, its lowest vote in any region of Spain (Culla, 2017: 278). Thereafter, in regions (including Euskadi and Galicia) with their own national tradition and a significant level of public questioning of the existing configuration of the Spanish state, occasional interference by the Podemos executive in local decision-making met strong resistance, with prominent figures abandoning the party.

A proportion of alternative left activists were now engaging simultaneously in pro-independence activities, while others preferred the idea of attempting to reconstitute Spain on a basis of shared sovereignty in the form of federalism or confederalism. In Catalonia, despite differences over the preferred 'territorial' formula, the vast majority of alternative left activists were united by Catalanism, that is, they envisaged their immediate national community as the primary context for political and social action and believed that democratic decisions taken therein should be fundamental, although they regarded collaboration with left-wing forces in other parts of Spain as essential to the pursuit of an agenda embracing social reform and constitutional change. Within Barcelona itself, with its own relatively small political ecosystem, it was clearly going to be easier to develop a project of left confluence than it would be across Spain as a whole, a country characterized by a system of multi-level government that requires parties operating electorally at different levels to balance between the demands emanating from the different constituencies involved.

One of BComú's other constituents, Iniciativa per Catalunya, had already asserted its autonomy of Spanish leadership by breaking its affiliation to Izquierda Unida back in the 1990s. A smaller participant, Esquerra Unida (EU), remained affiliated to IU, yet in the aftermath of the 15-M movement was seeking a new way of doing politics in Barcelona and more generally in Catalonia. In 2016, Podemos would eventually form an alliance with IU called 'United We Can' (Unidos Podemos, UP), in an attempt to achieve greater effectiveness in Spanish elections, but its electoral participation would take a different form in places where peripheral nationalisms had persisted through history: in communities such as Catalonia, Podemos had to accept the need to compete via autonomous left-wing *confluencias*.

Apart from the Catalan Greens, the parties that formed the ICV-EUiA alliance – which from November 2014 also included Comunistes de Catalunya, led by Joan Josep Nuet – had emerged from the traditional or 'classical' left through a process of supersession of the PSUC and had maintained ongoing associations with the old left by playing subordinate roles in PSC-headed administrations at regional and municipal level. Their eventual shift towards citizen-based politics was provoked by recent electoral setbacks suffered by the Socialists and by the massive size of the 15-M movement, which had surprised them, as had the growth of the CUP. Together, these developments presented them with an existential challenge. One reaction was to acknowledge their distance from Catalonia's dynamic social movements and from new, younger activists especially; another was to note the limited electoral appeal and potential of their own parties. Even ICV (Iniciativa per Catalunya Verds, Initiative for Catalonia Greens), which had emerged less damaged than the Socialists from the period of tripartite government, realized that its electoral alliance with EUiA (Esquerra Unida i Alternativa, United Left and Alternative) was never going to exceed 10–15 per cent of the votes at election time, even in those *barrios* where their core voters resided. Equally, they perceived the existence of a broad progressive majority in Catalan society that had yet to realize its political and electoral potential.

Although membership of these parties was low, the 15-M movement had demonstrated public interest in new forms of citizen politics. A growing number of Catalans were becoming involved in civil society activity to address problems, for example, through the creation of alternative energy cooperatives operating on a non-profit basis, rather than expecting solutions to be provided 'from above' by party leaders. The secondary parties of the established left saw new potential for change in Catalan society and recognized that it could only be harnessed through collaboration with social movement activists. They began to confer with such activists about how to establish a new 'political space' in which to engage in broader civilian-oriented collaboration and to build bridges between different sections of society with varying yet compatible demands for change.

Even so, there was a lingering tendency in the smaller left parties to conceive of this broader collaboration as being driven by a process of *party* alliance-building. Initially, it was the experience of the Coalition of the Radical Left (Syriza) in Greece that became the main point of reference for what they were trying to do in Catalonia. Indeed, ICV used the term 'Catalan Syriza' to describe their organizational goal, and active solidarity was engaged in with the party of Alexis Tsipras. The limits of a Syriza approach began to become apparent, however, in the Catalan election of 2012. Despite doing better than previously, ICV-EUiA with 9.9 per cent of the vote came fifth and now found itself challenged by the CUP, which had deputies elected for the first time. Some members of the allied parties concluded that a more fundamental change was needed: the creation of a citizen-based vehicle for political, social and institutional activity, described as the 'new political subject', thus avoiding the word 'party'. Moving in this direction would require conscious efforts to overcome remaining vestiges of sectarianism within the left and the doctrinaire mores that had tended to hamper outreach.

These political forces remained unresponsive to the upsurge of mobilization around territorial agendas promoted by the ANC (Assemblea Nacional Catalana, Catalan National Assembly) and Òmnium Cultural, along with independence parties. Constrained as they were by the federalist outlooks of many of their members, the most they could offer to broaden support in this direction was a strongly qualified endorsement of a Catalan 'right to decide' in a referendum; this, they insisted, should be achieved by legal and constitutional means, offer other territorial formulas besides independence and be used too to allow citizens a voice on fundamental social issues, thus avoiding a singular focus on independence. Their position left them distant from ERC although they envisaged cooperating with the Republican Left again after the territorial question was resolved or if Esquerra decided at some juncture to downplay it, as it had in 2003.

Meanwhile, splinters from the PSC (Partit dels Socialistes de Catalunya, Socialist Party of Catalonia), such as Ernest Maragall's Nueva Esquerra Catalana, would eventually find niches for themselves within pro-independence alliances. Thus, one can also speak of a process of 'confluence' around the independence issue, which, though partly a matter of party realignments, received much of its dynamism from civil society associations. The attraction of sectors of both the old and new left to this cause placed limits on the future potential of the new civilian-based political platform aspired to by the non-*independentista* alternative left. This would become a constraint once BComú was in office in Barcelona.

Entry of social movements into politics

The most striking feature of the Barcelona 'confluence' around the Comuns was the entry of people into political activity *for the first time*, although many of those involved had some history of protest and campaigning. By 2013, while eschewing the creation of a conventional party, these people were trying to find ways of making a political impact. One outcome was Procés Constituent, a political platform launched in April of that year by social movement activists and some senior citizens returning to campaign activity after a substantial interval, spurred by the opportunities that seemed to be opening up in Catalonia to change the status quo. With a view to the next Catalan elections, its aim was to present a unity ticket sponsored by all sections of the alternative left, to proclaim independence if it won and then to initiate a new constituent process, which it trusted would also bring socio-economic change, including the remunicipalization of public services in Barcelona. Once a Catalan constitution was established, it would then dissolve itself.

Procés attracted strong media attention owing to the leading role of Benedictine nun and social activist, Teresa Forcades, who headed the platform with fellow Catholic radical, Arcadi Oliveres. Several future leaders of the Comuns (Gerardo Pisarello, Jaume Asens, Xavier Domenèch) were also prominent in this movement, which attempted to transcend ideological differences and win public support transversally by emphasizing values such as decency and common sense. Procès was an intentionally transient movement that lost momentum in 2015, divided over whether to emphasize social transformation or Catalan independence (Martín López interview, 23 May 2018) and undermined by the emergence of Podemos and Guanyem Barcelona (the precursor to BComú) as well as scepticism on the part of the CUP. Its story added to a picture of great fluidity on the left, as activists strove for ways to become optimally organized and opted for platforms such as Procés and BComú that were non-doctrinaire and open to the involvement of individuals regardless of whether they maintained other political affiliations.

Social movement activists coming from the PAH (Plataforma de Afectados por la Hipoteca, Platform for Mortgage Victims) would be even more central to the rise of the Comuns, and here one must refer also to the Observatory on Economic, Social and Cultural Rights (DESC), based in Barcelona, which collaborated closely with it. Created in 1998, DESC had provided advice to people hit by home repossessions, offered training courses for activists and published reports on issues, such as the housing crisis and energy poverty. Colau herself worked there for seven years until 2015, and other members included her husband Adrià Alemany, Asens and Pisarello, the latter's partner Vanesa Valiño, and PAH activists, Gala Pin and Águeda Bañon. DESC was linked to the progressive tradition through being presided over by urban planner Jordi Borja, who had collaborated earlier with Pasqual Maragall and PSC-led municipal administrations.

Emphasizing the role of these organizations should not be allowed to obscure the diversity of entities with which founding members of BComú were involved previously. Many had been active in neighbourhood associations, not least the former president of the Federation of Barcelona Residents Associations (FAVB), Lluís Rabell. Others came from coordinating bodies such as the Alliance against Energy Poverty or were committed to municipal change in areas relating to their professional activities or intellectual interests. Cyberactivists committed to campaign organizations or with a prime interest in digital rights would feature too and their importance gradually became evident from the comparative advantage that the Comuns would enjoy over rival parties in respect of both internal and external communications. New communications technologies were fully harnessed and exploited by the Comuns, whose interaction with social networks would allow them to reach more extensively into society than the traditional parties.

Mention should be made too of the Institut de Govern i Polítiques Públiques (IGOP) at the Autonomous University of Barcelona, headed by Joan Subirats, whose members had advised previous Barcelona administrations on policy and became involved with them as a result of their expertise and political orientations. IGOP was also the professional base for the ICV group leader on the city council, Ricard Gomà, another key person in the creation of BComú.

The original core activists were already significant actors in civil society, extensively networked and often with dozens of other contacts whom they could call upon to collaborate, each with their own expertise and networks. Several, such as Gala Pin, were involved in multiple campaigning organizations and activities, including the cooperative movement, neighbourhood associations, civil rights groups and action groups concerned with the adverse effects of mass tourism on city residents.

One thing that the constituent groups and individuals all agreed upon was the importance and feasibility of making an immediate political impact, by trying to *win* an important election in the Catalan capital, rather than pursuing a more gradualist strategy. The ambition was expressed succinctly in the name chosen for the platform, *Guanyem Barcelona*, which translates as 'Let's Win Barcelona!' Later, differences would emerge over how the process of confluence should develop, with Podemos – especially at the Catalan level – tending to stick to a traditional mode of coalition-building driven by elite-level negotiations seeking compromise between existing programmes and priorities; the Guanyem activists closest to Ada Colau in BComú meanwhile would continue to advocate a more 'horizontal' approach to collaboration whereby a common political project was to be defined and developed by individuals collectively. The underlying aim was to create a citizens' platform that would be more than the sum of its parts (Guanyem Barcelona, 2014).

Here, Colau's group had some characteristics in common with the CUP, whose origins date from the 1980s (Fernàndez and De Jòdar, 2016). However, it disagreed with them over the possibility and desirability of taking control of state political institutions by means of an audacious immediate electoral assault. Besides possessing a longer-standing muni-cipalist orientation, the CUP emphasized the limited power of local government institutions in a neo-liberal world and was engaged in a deliberately long-term struggle to create popular power at the local level. Only after acquiring a strong presence within a community, through local agitation, occupations and the building of cooperatives, did the *cupaires* contemplate standing in local or Catalan elections, a matter to be decided by local assemblies. Dismissive of the view of institutional action as potentially decisive for societal transformation, CUP candidates elected to institutions saw their role as being to promote popular action in society to undermine the existing order. Regarding themselves as the 'Zapatistas of southern Europe', they did not believe in liberal-democratic electoral politics and suspected that BComú's initiative would amount to little more than 'a reconfiguration of social democratic Maragallism' (Fernàndez interview, 6 April 2017). Colau was to criticize the 'movementism' of the CUP and entered the electoral fray with a different mindset, determined to seek support in the centre as well as appeal to disadvantaged sectors (Serra Carné, 2016: 81). Nonetheless, the CUP was now becoming a significant actor within as well as outside the political institutions of Catalonia and the fact that it was not an automatic partner for the Comuns raised questions about the potential of the new platform to command majorities. Particularly in Barcelona, the CUP was noted for ideological rigidity and factionalism, which affected its ability to compromise with other sectors of the alternative left.

Taking the political initiative

More than a year of informal consultations and meetings between individuals and component groups eventually led to more definite planning of a collective political initiative in 2013–2014. On the way, high-profile social movement activists such as Colau, Pisarello and Pin had declined invitations from left-wing parties to join their electoral lists for the European elections of 2014 or the municipal elections a year later. They eventually decided to prioritize the municipal level of intervention. Several specific features of the Barcelona scene influenced this decision:

- the city's tradition of centre-left government;
- the vitality of its civil society and social movements;
- a business-friendly incumbent whose administration had neglected the poorer *barrios* of the city, yet who was to leave a financial surplus;
- a relatively low level of municipal indebtedness;

- the existence of a large enough budget (€2.5 billion in 2014) to permit contemplation of a far-reaching social agenda;
- a city at the heart of a major metropolitan area, where parties of the left had also been dominant;
- an important city in relation to global networks.

Colau's own decisions, to move on from social movements to political activity and to prioritize the municipal level, have been described as a catalyst of the process of confluence (Gomà interview, 11 November 2016). Owing to her high public profile, popularity, communication skills and integrity, and long before the actual process of electoral preparation began, she was widely recognized by other activists as the obvious person to head a list that had real prospects of success. With no baggage of party affiliation from her past, she was politically acceptable to all those wanting to create something new. Any other leadership candidates, if from a party, would have provoked disagreements and were never considered.

By this time, Colau had concluded that no social movement could change social conditions fundamentally. Ultimately the PAH had not achieved the kinds of legislative reforms it aimed for. Local government also had evident limits to its potential to instigate social change, but it did seem to have – among other things – the potential to slow the pace of home repossessions and increase the stock of social housing from an abysmally low historical level. However, Colau's move into politics, together with other social movement activists, was not so much a matter of 'going beyond' such movements as of trying to *transfer* a number of their positive attributes to the political arena: pragmatic concentration on specific, realizable goals rather than attempting comprehensive change all at once; 'transversalism' in the sense of seeking to be as socially inclusive as possible in building support for reform; and a horizontal way of doing things through collective forms of decision-making that set out to avoid hierarchy. The Comuns envisaged the PAH and other social movements as remaining crucial agents of change going forward, through applying pressure on a future left-wing administration. BComú would aspire to a 'co-production with an active citizenry', involving both institution-level action and social activism (Serra Carné, 2016: 88), the key to which would be mechanisms to establish interaction between citizens and institutional actors on an ongoing basis.

In 2013–2014, the consultations leading to the new initiative involved some 200 people. The proposal to create Guanyem Barcelona was presented by Colau, Asens and Subirats at a public meeting in a school in the *barrio* of El Raval in June 2014, attended by 400 people. Broad ideas to underpin the new platform were proposed at this juncture:

- certain basic rights for all;
- social and environmental justice;
- democratization of local government by holding municipal consultations of citizens between elections,
- auditing officials strictly and combatting corruption;
- an ethical code to increase the accountability of elected representatives by limiting terms of office, making accounts public and introducing recall mechanisms (Tugas, 2014: 215–216).

What was fresh about this initiative was that, following initial conversations among the promoters, the task of designing the new project was opened to public involvement, through the organization of groups at the *barrio* level, public meetings and the use of new social media. To test public reactions to the ideas that were now finding a consensus among core activists, the new platform set itself the goal of collecting 30,000 endorsements, at least half of them in the city of Barcelona itself. This was achieved ahead of a three-month deadline set by the promoters, through visiting various *barrios* of the city to seek support and by using sympathetic social networks.

Meanwhile, contact with existing organizations of the left, which was already occurring spontaneously in places, now took the form of more structured talks involving Guanyem, ICV, EUiA, the CUP, Procés Constituent and Podemos. The central idea was to take part in the municipal elections of May 2015 by means of a common platform, using the name Guanyem Barcelona. Formal commitment to a confluence process came almost immediately from ICV and EUiA, whereas the CUP remained critical and decided against participation, at least in Barcelona itself. Thereafter, the design of the project took place simultaneously through talks between members of different political groups and in public forums involving ordinary people, many becoming involved in a political process for the first time. Discussion revolved around the programme, an ethical code and the composition of the electoral list to be presented the following May.

By avoiding ideological discussion, concentrating on key issues of public concern and proceeding consensually whenever possible (rather than simply voting on different options), solid foundations were laid for the new platform in a deliberately gradual fashion. The integration of activists belonging to existing parties was potentially the greatest challenge, especially in the case of veterans who straddled the divide between old politics and new. Yet this was managed effectively by insisting that people could only participate as individuals, with nobody being regarded as more important than anyone else; moreover there would be no requirement that members should prioritize Guanyem activity over any other party commitments, thus minimizing any difficulties over conflicting loyalties (Salado interview, 11 November 2016). This was a formula that, in the short to medium term at least, worked well for all: those around Colau who had created Guanyem and who hoped that ultimately the confluence process would result in the complete transcendence of the parties backing the project; and those in left parties who valued both confluence and the continuing development of their own party.

Notwithstanding the achievement of programmatic consensus and complete unity over Colau's leadership, the new platform exhibited some characteristics of a coalition. On the one hand, in the short term at least, there existed an inner network of activists who were close to Colau as a result of the effectiveness of earlier collaboration, especially through the PAH and DESC. When future debates occurred, those most closely associated with her, the confidantes of the mayor, would continue to be referred to in the media as 'Colau's group' or as 'Guanyem', even after the broader confluence platform was launched with the same name, and after February 2015, when it was renamed Barcelona en Comú. 'Guanyem' would have an afterlife as a distinct political culture and network, alongside those of partner organizations (Shea Baird interview, 21 May 2018). On the other hand, the old parties continued to maintain a parallel existence in the stratosphere of the Comuns. In time, many activists who arrived via existing parties did come to prioritize the collective project (De Maya interview, 3 April 2017; Nuet interview, 6 April 2017), but only Procés Constituent – another platform rather than a party – was to disappear completely from the scene as BComú became consolidated.

Within the pre-existing parties of Leninist descent, it was considered by some that their internal discipline would allow them to contribute an element of stability to the 'new political subject', given that the Guanyem platform also attracted many who were fresh to political activity or at least had no experience of government or institutional involvement. A minority of EUiA members remained unconvinced by the confluence strategy in any case, and their views needed to be borne in mind by their leaders (Nuet interview, 6 April 2017). ICV, which made a fundamental contribution to establishing the new platform ahead of the municipal elections by advancing funds from subsidies it had qualified for through earlier involvement in elections and institutions, as well as donating its quota of access to public communications media and making its infrastructure available, continued to believe that certain aspects of its record in office were positive and that its members could now contribute valuable experience to the municipal administration formed in 2015 (Cid interview, 9 November 2016; Gomà interview, 11 November 2016). More open than EUiA to the possibility of eventual disbandment, it would later, in July 2019, announce its intention to dissolve: a decision hastened by approaching insolvency.

When it came to discussion of the electoral list, political balance together with a desire to present a solid, convincing city governance team led eventually to the presentation of a closed list in the BComú primaries, negotiated by the participating political forces, rather than an open list allowing preferences for individual candidates to be influential (Serra Carné, 2016: 90). More than 3,000 people endorsed it. The only competitive primaries held were for district councillors (officially to be appointed by the mayor) and these proved to be somewhat divisive, with those who lost often returning to their social movement activities (Martín López interview, 23 May 2018). The main political forces were all present among the 11 BComú candidates elected ultimately, 3 coming from Guanyem, 3 from ICV, 4 from Podem and 1 from EUiA (Culla, 2017: 282). Besides this political pluralism, the list possessed a high proportion of people with professional skills or policy specializations relating to the programmatic agenda that was being mapped out (for example, urban planners, environmental activists and housing specialists). While the lead position (Colau) had been uncontroversial, there was some argument about the second place, to which ICV felt strongly entitled. Others, not least those wishing to avoid a traditional alliance approach, resisted and eventually Pisarello was chosen by consensus. He had joined Guanyem from Procés Constituent but was involved in diverse activities and thus was seen as a non-partisan figure (Mir Garcia interview, 8 April 2017).

Also proving internally controversial was the platform's code of ethics finalized in October 2014 and seen as a priority, to endow the platform with stricter safeguards against corruption than those found in the old parties. Key principles were to avoid professionalization in order to maintain the citizen-based model of engagement in political life, to counter the creation of privileged political elites or 'revolving doors' between politics and business by limiting salaries and to provide recall mechanisms to encourage accountability. Measures finally adopted for BComú representatives in institutions were:

- the limitation of consecutive terms of office to two (or exceptionally three, following a consultation of members);
- a salary limit set at three times the minimum wage;

- complete transparency concerning the finances of BComú and the administrations it controlled, with information being made more readily available to the public.

During the early phases of discussion, the ethical code had been a sticking point for the involvement of the CUP, whose own code was even more stringent, limiting elected representatives to just one term of office. From an opposing viewpoint, the code was resisted too, initially, by ICV. For the eco-socialists, the proposed limitation on terms of office in practice meant the exclusion from the 2015 electoral list of its municipal leader Ricard Gomà as well as the departure of experienced politicians Jaume Bosch and Dolors Camats from the Catalan Parliament, to which they had been elected originally in 2003. ICV also voiced concerns that limiting net salaries of political representatives to €2,200 a month (with the surplus being contributed to BComú or any constituent party) might make it difficult to recruit highly qualified professionals to public office in an elected or appointed capacity. Gomà's willingness to sacrifice his own political career to facilitate the confluence process helped overcome this stumbling block, but it did leave some ICV members feeling that he had been badly treated.

Guanyem was being organized on a horizontal basis of *barrio* groups, *barrio* and district assemblies, a coordinating body, committees and working groups with a functional or thematic focus. The platform's initial coordinating body, while not officially based on political quotas, did have a minimum number of people from each organization. In the longer term, however, as the organizational structure of the platform developed, party affiliations increasingly gave way to consideration of the individual qualities of candidates (Salado interview, 11 November 2016) and the desire for team coherence. The organization would be further elaborated and developed in the summer of 2015, when BComú adopted a more party-like structure, with an executive as well as a coordinating committee, and acquired some full-time and part-time employees (notably Alemany), although a lot of work continued to be done by activists. Particularly during the drafting of the electoral programme, a wide range of expertise was drawn upon through the thematic groups, open to anyone interested in developing policy in a particular area. Providing flexibility, supporters could become involved at whatever level they wished: through a *barrio* group meeting regularly, through online involvement with thematic groups, or just occasionally, notably during the election campaign. The party's funding also depended on crowd-sourcing – one-off or regular donations, or micro-loans for repayment to individuals after the election – since both membership subscriptions (a barrier to participation) and bank loans were ruled out on principle.

The change of name to BComú may have caused some confusion among voters and certainly left little time for the new name to be established among the electorate in time for the municipal elections, but a change of this kind was forced upon the platform by the registration of the name Guanyem by a councillor from another party. In fact, the change proved fortuitous. 'Guanyem' had some advantages: insisting on the possibility and importance of winning; putting the emphasis on citizens 'winning back' control of the city and a series of rights deemed to have been undermined by the austerity drive undertaken by the old parties (Colau, 2015). Yet what lasting value would it have had following its first electoral contest? 'Barcelona en Comú' lacked this disadvantage, it underlined that the initiative was a collective and inclusive one and made reference to the idea of 'commons' that influenced some leading figures theoretically and yet could be understood too at a non-theoretical level and thus was meaningful to a large number of activists and potential voters, who were not familiar with this line of thought. Equally, by including Barcelona in the title, it postulated the importance of the city as an important site for achieving social change and responding to globalization.

Faced with the need to establish itself vis-à-vis the electorate in just a few months before the election, BComú used the same tactic as Podemos in the European elections, by placing a photograph of its leader on the ballot papers as well as in electoral publicity. This certainly ran contrary to the horizontal approach and collective leadership principle that Guanyem had embraced and risked accusations of personalism from rivals whose lists continued to use established party logos. It did not prove controversial within BComú, however, given the lack of time to establish the brand and explain the project. Colau had become a well-known face and respected figure through her role in the PAH and for many that experience had shown how valuable an articulate leader could be to a movement. She was a very significant electoral asset in her own right. A poll in July 2014 showed her to be the most popular of the likely candidates for mayor and the one with the greatest transversal appeal, extending to all but PP and Ciudadanos (Cs, Citizens) voters (*El Periódico*, 25 July 2014). Colau herself was not keen on her image being on the ballot paper (Serra Carné, 2016: 89–90). She was not the kind of leader who dominated decision-making discussions but rather was noted for listening to the views of others, sometimes being persuaded by them and not insisting on having the final word (Cid interview, 9 November 2016; Mir Garcia interview, 8 April 2017).

Colau was to criticize Podemos publicly for excessive personalism, yet the Comuns themselves at least came to see the establishment of a strong public figure as essential to effective political communication and realized that 'Ada' had rare qualities that enabled the diverse political components of BComú to work together. Apart from being an emblem of the 15-M movement, she was appreciated as a builder of consensus and for being receptive to good ideas even when coming from individuals who earlier had been involved in the 'old' politics.

Podemos was to prove more divided than the other parties in BComú, and its anti-capitalist current especially was insistent on maintaining a distinctive political brand and demanded a high proportion of the leadership positions when the Comuns proceeded to develop a confluence process at the Catalan level. However, in Barcelona itself, the prominent role of erstwhile social movement activists, the inclusive way in which the platform was built, the personal recognition of Colau and BComú by Pablo Iglesias as equivalents of Podemos in their specific municipal context, the relative weakness of Podemos in the city and the Comuns' achievement of immediate electoral success all facilitated the integration of activists associated with Podem. At the city level, they joined Guanyem/BComú as individuals, as 'believers in a shared project' (Mir Garcia interview, 8 April 2017). At the wider Catalan level, the process would be more complicated.

Ideas of the Comuns

It would be wrong to present the Comuns as a new party with a clear ideological orientation. Even though BComú's legal status was that of an electoral party, the Comuns remained sceptical about parties and the capacity of the state alone to achieve a thoroughgoing transformation of society in a neo-liberal global context. Some members saw BComú as simply a vehicle for getting radical activists into office in order to change the direction of policy and open up the political system to citizen participation, which implied a rather transitory life for the platform itself. They had no notion of building a conventional party, relying instead on a more ad hoc approach to mobilizing supporters in order to wage campaigns, especially at election times. Others in BComú attached more importance to the building of an expanding activist base, particularly those with a longer-term perspective of seeking to achieve a lasting progressive hegemony (for example, Domènech, 2016). BComú's organizational distinction, between *activistas* (those attending meetings and making a contribution to local or thematic groups) and *inscritos* (those registered with the organization and involved mostly via periodic online consultations) had the flexibility to accommodate both visions as well as individual preferences, but it left a lot of questions about the future of the platform and its capacity to contribute to change from within society.

Militants joining the confluence process from parties of the alternative left had more demanding standards of activism but brought no new ideological stimulus. The relatively new ideas that influenced the politics of BComú were identified more with academics and activists coming from social movements. The latter embraced the concept of 'commons', currently enjoying considerable currency in various strands of the anti-globalization movement. This did not involve an attempt to develop a systematic ideology or a dogmatic approach. Indeed, these people were open to collaboration with others on a common project that would always be a 'work in progress' and they shared the propensity of the Comuns in general to concentrate on immediate and practical objectives.

Already present in the early years of Europe's experience of democratization, among movements such as the seventeenth-century Diggers in England, the idea of 'commons' had received fresh impetus from the invention of the Internet. In the political sphere, this had prompted renewed debates about how democracy might be extended in a more direct fashion, about ways of sharing goods and experiences, the use of horizontal communication platforms for campaign purposes and cooperative economic activity. In Spain, such debates attracted more interest from 2011 as widespread criticism of the political parties translated, during the great recession, into a crisis of representative democracy, with many people echoing the 15-M slogan, 'They don't represent us', referring to politicians. Even in this context, the influence of theories of the commons remained restricted to very few people, but specific applications of the concept in ideas about digital or cultural rights had somewhat wider resonance.

For those influenced by writers such as Elinor Ostrom, David Bollier, Michael Hardt and Antonio Negri, the main political significance of commons thinking was that, compared with the social democratic era, strategic approaches to the attainment of societal transformation could – and indeed now needed to be – less reliant on the state. The very limited ability of social democratic parties to effect social change in the face of global market forces was no longer a compelling reason for the left to resign itself to social liberal policies (although part of the left continued to do so). Commons thinking suggested that cooperation could be built decisively within civil society, beginning at the local level, where traditional rights could be reclaimed and reasserted and inequalities challenged. The empowerment of citizens was to be key to changing the recent subordination of political institutions to the market.

The main expositor of such thinking in Catalonia was the political scientist, Joan Subirats, a professor at the Autonomous University of Barcelona, who was to become one of the three spokespersons of Guanyem Barcelona in 2014. In *Otra sociedad, ¿otra política?* (2011), Subirats discussed the changes in society brought about by the Internet and the global financial crisis and pointed to a contradiction in Spain between new economic and societal circumstances and an antiquated political system. Markets and economic power had become global, yet political institutions remained anchored at the territorial level, where the adverse effects of globalization were being felt and states had shown little capacity to act upon them decisively. Democracy in Spain had been hollowed out, both by globalizing market forces and by regional devolution. With reference to the 15-M, Subirats argued that a new social space had emerged in which action and collaboration could take place, replacing strategies based on the traditional dilemma of market versus state. The Internet linked society, globally. A different, more horizontal way of doing politics was now possible through the creation of citizen-based platforms that would enable activism to be linked and operationalized by means of Internet discussion and consultation, while also using local assemblies.

This was not an espousal of direct democracy, but rather of participative democracy, a 'democracy of the commons', to complement the institutions of representative democracy. Nonetheless, Subirats did posit a need to change the existing political system as a prerequisite for achieving social objectives. His democratic advocacy raised issues of equality as well. The Internet provided new opportunities to organize and act on a non-hierarchical basis, in the collaborative construction of common goods and the defence of common rights; it could be used to involve the general public more in collective affairs, although existing centres of power would continue to have great influence. Subirats was not suggesting that the new would replace the old entirely. Rather, an alternative to the existing order characterized by hierarchy and competition was envisaged, based on participation and collaboration; it would develop alongside the old structures and indeed seek to use some market mechanisms and the state to serve its purposes. Equally, political parties would continue to have useful functions; they should remain in existence, but not be allowed to monopolize the decision-making process. Parties themselves were already seeking ways of strengthening their contact and interaction with citizens.

Aware of the risks of technologically-empowered manipulation, Subirats emphasized the need for adequate processes of public deliberation before consultations of citizens took place, yet wanted such mechanisms to become systemic features, forming part of an ongoing process rather than remaining ad hoc. He acknowledged the doubts expressed by some social scientists about the feasibility of a more participative democracy (limits to the interest of citizens in issues not directly affecting them, the technical complexity surrounding some issues) and the use of the Internet (for example, inequality of access), yet thought that the difficulties should be embraced as challenges for a new democratizing politics since citizens had become so alienated from the existing system (Subirats, 2011: 64–65).

Commons thinking was rooted in the idea of common goods that could not be owned but could be maintained and regulated by the community. The Internet could facilitate developments in this direction by reducing the costs of connection and interaction, allowing peer-to-peer exchanges free from the involvement of market or state, which could be used to address common areas of need via the sharing of information, culture and knowledge. Political facilitation would come through developing a civilian-oriented participative politics, involving a confluence of forces that would include elements from the classical left. It was acknowledged that, beyond the old anarcho-syndicalist tradition, cooperative approaches to economic activity had tended to be seen by the left in Spain as possessing somewhat marginal value; even within the cooperative movement, which had been relatively strong in Catalonia, there had been a somewhat sceptical response to the recent debates about commons (Subirats and Rendueles, 2016: 59–61). Nonetheless, the idea of developing mutualism further was one that would feature quite prominently in the BComú programme. This is something that finds parallels in the CUP, but they had been creating cooperatives from the bottom up, rather than looking partly to institutional action to facilitate them.

The change of name from Guanyem to Barcelona en Comú, chosen in preference to alternatives such as 'Confluence for Barcelona' and 'Democratic Spring', brought the concept of commons into the public identity of the new platform. However, it would always serve in a dual fashion, both as a mark of ideational identity and to denote the idea of acting through a confluence of forces and citizens wanting to do politics in a more horizontal way and thus modify existing forms of representation. The notion of the commons was compatible with the pre-existing ecological and feminist orientations of the alternative left, which already drew on the concept to some extent. Both environmentalism and feminism would feature as mainstream currents in the outlook of the Comuns, perhaps even more strongly than commons thinking itself. Commitment to a green agenda was fuelled by

Barcelona's particularly acute pollution problems. The feminist outlook reflected the prominent role of women in the social movements. BComú argues that its feminism makes it less adversarial than the classical left, through a belief in convincing rather than imposing and an eminently practical approach to problems. It sees *despatriarcalizació* as an ongoing challenge for the organization itself, a key to developing a more horizontal form of leadership that is 'empathetic and collaborative'. Feminist commitment is expressed both through policy and in the way the Comuns organize and operate, from the organization of crèche facilities and admission of offspring at meetings to the adoption of norms of alternation and parity between men and women in the conduct of meetings and positions of leadership and representation (Barcelona en Comú, 2017: 12; Caymel interview, 7 April 2017; Roth interview, 8 November 2016; Shea Baird interview, 21 May 2018; Pérez interview, 12 April 2019).

There was no phase of conceptual discussion within the new platform before it was launched: rather, any debates around commons remained confined to an erudite minority of those involved in the new project, who in time would gradually engage with a larger number of activists through 'La Comuna', a forum for debate within Guanyem which became the BComú training school. There is little evidence that the currency of the conceptual thinking extends beyond a proportion of the activists. One obstacle may be the lack of an accessible handbook outlining the ideas clearly, simply and with reference to the local and Catalan contexts. The publication in Barcelona of a very dense 669-page French work in 2015 made no difference in this regard, even for the purposes of schooling BComú activists (Laval and Dardot, 2015; Subirats interview, 7 April 2017).

In practice, BComú has been able to accommodate both those who are influenced by commons thinking and a much larger number who are unfamiliar with it, yet who readily identify with the policy proposals that have been influenced by its premises. Colau herself, although in touch with the conceptual debates, has taken no part in them in public but rather has stuck to practical applications and common-sense notions in her discourse.

The circumscribed role of ideology during the rise of Barcelona en Comú reflects the fact that it was born out of a confluence over a short period of time, under pressure from the electoral calendar. In the end, the new platform was perceived as threateningly radical by conservatives but as unconvincing by the far left. The CUP regards the Comuns' 'lack of a clear ideology' as a weakness, leading to political inconsistency in office and deep ambiguity over the question of Catalan independence (Rovira interview, 9 November 2016). A much older movement, the CUP adheres to more systematic ideological positions, although it embraces several different tendencies. BComú activists acknowledge that their initial approach was characterized by short-termism, some expecting that a longer-term perspective would emerge when they proceeded to create the 'new political subject' at the Catalan level (Salado interview, 11 November 2016). In fact, the creation of Catalonia en Comú in 2016–2017 would also be a process whose pace was hurried by electoral exigencies and did not add to the ideological definition of the confluence.

'Winning back the city'

BComú's victory in the municipal elections of 2015 was not something widely expected. In the months beforehand, many commentators saw the main challenge to the incumbent CiU, again led by Trias, as coming from ERC. CiU's prospects were affected by ongoing economic dissatisfaction, adverse criticism of Trias for his handling of the squatter occupation of a building named Can Vies and the tax scandal enveloping former Catalan government president Jordi Pujol. ERC, as the more unequivocal pro-independence party, stood to make gains owing to rising support for a separate Catalan state, as did the CUP. However, with the division of the pro-independence vote spread across three parties and the pro-independence issue not perceived as decisive in the city's municipal election, the contest in Barcelona eventually became one between CiU and the Comuns and ultimately between Trias and Colau. A secondary competition took place between the three unionist parties, the PSC, PP and Cs.

BComú set out to polarize the contest between itself and the incumbent, presenting Trias as a defender of the status quo whose spending policies had ignored the poorer *barrios* of the city. The Comuns made a special effort to mobilize there, in districts such as Nou Barris and Sant Martí, and amplified their campaign by involving neighbourhood and social movement activists and all sympathetic social networks. Even their rivals recognized that they ran a very effective campaign, both on the ground and through the web, making best use of a clear discourse promising change, with their lead candidate lending credibility to that promise. What was particularly distinctive about the BComú electoral list was the prominent position of women. Recent struggles over home evictions and other social issues had drawn many women into activism; the prominence in the list of strong female figures associated with those struggles would now encourage further support from women for a platform that aimed to feminize political life. The electoral list was certainly short on governmental experience, but demonstrated a strong commitment to ending male dominance in political life. Of the 11 BComú candidates elected, 6 were women and among them both Colau and Pin were outstanding protagonists of social movement campaigning. Another two (from ICV) had political experience: Laia Ortiz, a former member of the Spanish Congress of Deputies noted for anti-poverty initiatives, and Janet Sanz, the one person to have served already on the city council, specializing in environmental issues (Shea Baird, 2015). On a wider scale, the municipal elections would increase greatly the number of women mayors of differing party affiliations in greater Barcelona, in cities with a combined population of 2.4 million (*El País*, 28 February 2016).

The electoral programme was drafted in an inclusive manner, open to inputs from interested members of the public. Discussion began among core political activists before proceeding to involve over 5,000 people, 20 *barrio* assemblies and 2,500 contributions during the second half of 2014 (Serra Carné, 2016: 98). The document was divided into two sections: one thematically organized, setting out specific measures and indicating the prioritization that had been made in the citizen-focused participative process; the other reflecting the specific demands that had been made in each of the city's ten districts. The programme promised a continuous process of monitoring policy performance through the creation of an autonomous municipal observatory involving experts and citizens, whose work would be made visible through the municipal website (Barcelona en Comú, 2015).

The document can be summarized by reference to its four thematic sections:

1 *Basic Rights* envisaged plans to reduce inequalities and promote rights: measures to reduce home evictions and provide alternative accommodation when these proved unavoidable; guarantees of basic food and energy provision to those affected by poverty, for whom a 'municipal income' was promised; efforts to ensure the access of migrants to health services; and measures to promote employment and diversify economic activity.

2 *Change of Model* aimed at counteracting trends towards privatization, job insecurity and segregation. Specifics here included the use of municipal contracts to ensure compliance with social and environmental standards; the prioritization of investment in poor *barrios*; support for SMEs, partly through the creation of a local currency; a moratorium on the concession of licences for tourist flats; efforts to secure a bigger share of the tourist tax from the Generalitat and to involve citizens in deciding how to use it; a

halting of luxury projects; steps towards the re-municipalization of water provision; the development of a more sustainable integrated system of public transport; the promotion of renewable energy, partly via the creation of a new provider; anti-pollution measures, including support for cycling; migration by the council towards free software and open access; support for social housing through housing cooperatives; the extension of cultural and civic centres; the mainstreaming of gender equality in all policy areas; and initiatives addressing violence against women and phobias affecting LBGTI communities.

3   *City for Life* set out proposals aiming to tackle differences in the quality of life between different *barrios* and social sectors of the city. Included here were an expansion of primary health care provision, plans to municipalize home-help services, defence of the Catalan language as a vehicle of integration and coexistence, pressure for the closure of the state-run migrant detention centre in the city and more assistance for asylum seekers.

4   Finally, *Open Democracy* was where plans for political transformation were presented: municipal decentralization by making *barrio* councils a more effective channel for local demands; steps towards the direct election of district councillors; the involvement of citizens in decisions via consultations, citizen initiatives (with a reduced signature threshold requirement), auditing procedures and recall mechanisms; a new secure system for Internet-based consultations; the earmarking of funding for priorities proposed directly by citizens (following Reykjavik); public debates about big investment decisions; the creation of independent citizens councils selected by lottery, to debate issues and express views; initiatives to integrate migrants in participatory processes; the creation of a municipal anti-corruption office; and the promotion of youth councils.

This programme amounted to quite radical reform in the context of Barcelona, especially through its emphasis on the re-municipalization of services, measures to involve citizens in governance, the mainstreaming of women's rights and redistributive policies. It was not constrained by a narrow interpretation of municipal jurisdiction even where the main competence was fixed constitutionally at the state and/ or regional level: the aim was to bring change even in areas such as housing, social policy, health and education. City representation on the boards of consortia managing shared-competence areas of service provision, along with negotiation, lobbying and pressure, would be used to influence policy decisions at higher levels. This entailed the risk that the city administration might be held publicly responsible for shortfalls even when the legal jurisdiction was located partly or wholly elsewhere. Opposition parties would certainly attribute all shortfalls to Colau and the Comuns, regardless of the distribution of competences.

A further complication for the mandate being sought was the confinement of the Comuns primarily to the city of Barcelona. BComú had counterparts in several other municipalities of the metropolitan area, but these were formed generally by confluences with different components to BComú, or by ICV-EUiA. The governing body of the area would see an eventual balance between left confluences with six seats, the PSC six and ERC two. Thus, the future of metropolitan-based services would continue to be influenced by a range of parties.

In the election, the detailed programme was arguably less important than a vague feeling that Colau would bring change whereas the others would not (Pedret interview, 10 November 2016). The level of public interest was shown in a 7.6 per cent increase in participation, which reached 60.6 per cent. BComú won in six of the ten districts of the city, taking five from the PSC and one from CiU, which won in the other four. The Comuns especially celebrated their 33.8 per cent of the vote in Nou Barris, where the poorest *barrios* were concentrated, and this proved crucial to the outcome. There, a particularly radical message helped to mobilize voters, raising participation from 47.6 to 55.5 per cent. CiU meanwhile suffered from the division of the *independentista* vote and growing support for more unequivocal independence parties. Even so, it was a disappointing election for ERC as well, following its victory here in the 2014 European elections; it was even outpolled by the unionist Cs, which won seats for the first time. Overall the Catalan independence issue proved less decisive than debate about the social model of the city, although the contrast was not so clear-cut: Trias personally had played down the territorial question (fearing that it would alienate his more conservative supporters) but parties supporting 'the right to decide' (BComú, CiU, ERC, CUP) were now in the majority, with 28 seats out of the 41, 11 more than in 2011 (Table 3.1).

The result produced a council that was more fragmented than in 2011–2015, with 7 parties/alliances represented, compared with 5 previously and the winning list having just 11 out of 41 seats, as opposed to 14 earlier. BComú had only about half the elected councillors that most previous victors had been able to form their administrations with. Moreover, the central government had cut the number of political appointments (advisors, experts, heads of cabinet and press officers) that could be made in city hall from 166 to 92, of which the Comuns' negotiated share would be 49 (*El País*, 8 July 2019). Although this did

Table 3.1 Results of the municipal election in Barcelona, 2015

Party	Votes	(%)	Seats	Variation*
BComú	176,612	25.1	11	+6**
CiU	159,393	22.7	10	-4
Cs	77,272	11.0	5	+5
ERC	77,120	11.0	5	+3
PSC	67,489	9.6	4	-7
PP	61,004	8.7	3	-7
CUP	51,945	–	3	+3

Source: Ajuntament de Barcelona www.bcn.cat/estadistica/angles/dades/telec/loc/locevo/clocev01.htm

Notes: *compared with seats won in 2011; **compared with ICV-EUiA in 2011.

not necessitate the negotiation of a coalition government, it at least meant that partners would need to be found for the approval of new budgets and for key aspects of the Programme for Municipal Action (PAM), which would serve as the new administration's road map. Trias had governed through agreements with the PSC and PP. Colau would seek support from ERC, the PSC and the CUP.

4 Party politics under a radical minority government

Ada Colau was sworn in as the first female mayor of Barcelona in June 2015. She headed the smallest administration in her city's history under democracy. The Comuns had just 11 out of the 41 council members and since no immediate coalition proved possible, each of their councillors had to take responsibility for a broad policy area and for one of the 10 municipal districts. Votes from ERC (Esquerra Republicana de Catalunya, Republican Left of Catalonia) and the PSC (Partit dels Socialistes de Catalunya, Socialist Party of Catalonia) and more stinting help from the CUP (Candidatura d'Unitat Popular, Popular Unity Candidature) would facilitate Colau's investiture, but the early BComú efforts to negotiate a coalition were unproductive; and even when collaboration with the Socialists was agreed upon the following year, this did not deliver an overall majority on the city council and it proved short-lived. Over the four-year term of office, the Comuns thus relied heavily on negotiating piecemeal support from other parties for items on their agenda and generally needed help from at least two of them, either through their support or abstention. Given the political fragmentation of the council and differences in both ideological and constitutional positions between the parties, BComú was thus obliged (albeit less so during the coalition with the PSC) to resort to a strategy of variable geometry, turning to some parties for support on certain issues and to different parties on others. This involved some complicated conjuring acts that proved difficult to sustain over time for the vicissitudes of inter-party relations were affected greatly by electoral considerations among party representatives.

This was also a period that saw municipal politics in Barcelona become bound up increasingly with Catalan national politics. As the conflict over sovereignty permeated the city, it cut across the left-right political struggle and posed fresh questions for the project of enhanced democratic participation that had informed the outlook of the Comuns when they took office. Some of the allies that would be needed to put together a left-wing majority

(ERC, CUP) would try to commit the city to the cause of independence and quickly became critical of BComú's efforts to simply defend a 'right to decide' through some form of referendum. Parties to the right of the Comuns (the Partido Popular, People's Party, PP, Ciudadanos, Citizens, Cs, PSC) meanwhile opposed the radicalism of BComú's social agenda and/or criticized its ideas on civil empowerment. Colau and her team had expected their policies to be resisted by conservative forces, but they ended up being opposed more crucially by the pro-independence movement, with consequences for some key policies in the Comuns' programme. Notwithstanding the municipalist priorities of BComú, it proved impossible to avoid involvement in the evolving battle over Catalonia's relationship to Spain. Not only had public support for independence grown in Barcelona by 2015: the Comuns' initial advocacy of a referendum negotiated with central government was fast losing credibility owing to the refusal of the Rajoy government and most Spanish party political leaders to agree to a bilateral negotiation of the constitutional status of Catalonia.

Lacking experience in government, Colau's new administration was unable to hit the ground running. Inevitably, its first year in office was devoted to a stock-taking of inherited municipal practice and the conversion of the electoral programme into policy. Within months, it also found itself having to operate in a somewhat different Catalan political context following the victory of the new Junts pel Sí (JxSí) alliance in the September 2015 regional election, which eventually gave rise to a coalition government headed by Carles Puigdemont, with external support from the CUP. This new Catalan administration pressed hard for the authorities of the capital city Barcelona, as well as other municipalities, to collaborate over a road map that, if Madrid still refused to negotiate, would involve a unilateral process leading to a referendum.

Nonetheless, Colau's administration commenced its life in some favourable circumstances. It inherited a relatively strong financial position; minority government was by no means new to the city and traditionally had been facilitated – at least for inaugural purposes – by opposition parties; Barcelona's political system was strongly *alcaldista*, its mayor endowed with strong individual powers of decree; and BComú was well placed to survive a full term of office, given that other parties, owing to fragmentation and mutual vetoes, were incapable of assembling an overall majority to support an alternative mayoral candidate, as would be necessary if they were to pass a motion of no confidence to replace the incumbent.

This chapter discusses the party politics of Barcelona during the Colau administration of 2015–2019, leaving an overview of policy performance as the theme of Chapter 5. It examines the contours of political alignment and opposition that affected the delivery of the BComú programme. The analysis of inter-party dynamics falls into three phases: (1) an initial period of reliance on ad hoc agreements with other parties, made easier by a degree of collaborative disposition on the part of other parties of the left; (2) a subsequent period of formal coalition with the PSC, which brought more stability and took some of the workload from the shoulders of the BComú councillors; and (3) a final period of acute and damaging isolation as polarization over the independence issue deepened. Municipal party dynamics shifted in successive phases as debates about the direction to be taken by Barcelona – the Barcelona 'model' – were affected by electoral competition at other levels of government and as the municipal focus became overshadowed by controversies over the city's position in the deepening confrontation between the Catalan authorities and the central government in Madrid.

In office, but not in power

Following the May 2015 election, Ada Colau negotiated with both ERC and PSC about the possibility of a coalition or some lesser form of collaboration. Part of the difficulty lay in the fact that for the left-wing measures that characterized the BComú programme, multiple partners would be necessary, yet – in contrast to the Catalan coalition experience of 2003–2010 – it was virtually impossible to involve both ERC and the PSC in a coalition now that the former had come to focus primarily on the objective of Catalan independence whereas the latter belonged to the unionist camp, although wanting to see constitutional reform lead to a federal framework in which to accommodate Catalan sovereignty-based aspirations. Even if it had proved possible to form a coalition with these parties, Colau would still have needed assistance from other parties, at least through abstention, and the only one of these on the left was the firmly anti-system and pro-independence CUP with its inborn reluctance to participate in institutions and lack of vocation to govern; it agreed with part of the BComú programme but saw its overall stamp as social democratic. During the early negotiations, ERC – the preferred partner of the Comuns (Cid interview, 9 November 2016) – kept open the possibility of establishing an eventual coalition, yet insisted that this would need to exclude the Socialists and would require a substantial period of political discussion before agreement would be reached. Essentially, its Council leader, Alfred Bosch, was looking for reciprocity: practical commitments in relation to the independence road map in return for cooperation over social democratic measures (Alfred Bosch interview, 12 November 2016). In the meantime, ERC was willing to support the investiture of Colau as mayor and to negotiate over specific measures. The fact that important Catalan elections were just months away, in September, made any municipal coalition unlikely until these were over. This was an initial demonstration of how the Catalan dimension would impinge on the political process of the city even during the first phase.

Given its desires to reduce social inequality, break with the elitist model of democracy and thus remain consistent with alternative left principles, BComú did not expect or seek any more than occasional support from the centre-right parties. Opposition leader Xavier Trias, who himself had settled for a degree of policy continuity with the previous Socialist-led administration, was disappointed to find the Comuns uninterested in negotiations with CiU (Convergència i Unió, Convergence and Unity) and unconvinced by his argument that pragmatic compromise was key to ensure the success of any city policies that would take several successive administrations to implement and consolidate (Trias interview, 8 November 2016). BComú received occasional support from centre-right parties for a few housing and urban planning measures, but strategically its efforts to implement its programme depended on the support it could attract from other sectors of the left.

Colau's investiture on 15 June counted with the votes of the PSC and ERC as well as one of the three votes possessed by the CUP, without policy concessions being made in return. Her discourse was inclusive, expressing a desire to be mayor for 'all residents of the city', across all 73 of its *barrios*. The commitment to an inevitably controversial programme of radical reform, however, was indicated by the prominent presence of social movement activists at the ceremony in city hall and outside, in the Plaça de Sant Jaume, and in the well-publicized action of the new incumbent pinning to her office door a notice saying, 'Never forget who we are, or why we are here.' Nonetheless, the Comuns believed it was possible to achieve quite radical goals with the support of a progressive majority in society, and in pursuit of this Colau acted fairly pragmatically from the outset to broaden the base of her administration. Although policy agreements with rival parties often took many months to negotiate, outreach to other sectors of public opinion was possible from early on through the incorporation of suitably qualified people to fill positions in the city hall: a step seen as valuable in any case, given the inexperience of BComú. Perhaps the greatest political coup was the recruitment in June of the former leader of the Socialist municipal group, Jordi Martí, as municipal manager – the main executive officer for the administration itself, various autonomous bodies and municipal companies, also in charge of the budget and investment. Martí, who had substantial experience of public administration, had been a member of the PSC sector that upheld the idea of Catalan sovereignty before resigning from the party over this issue in 2014, having been defeated in primary elections by Jaume Collboni, now leader of the party's municipal group. Other former members of the Socialist Party, including some associated with the Maragall era, also brought experience to the Colau administration, whose use of appointments otherwise drew heavily on people who had collaborated with her in the social movement community and thus tended to be fresh to political office.

Negotiating majorities

If the achievements of the Colau administration were slow to emerge, this was because the Comuns wanted to take stock of existing policies and practices, and had a steep learning curve to climb, rather than because of opposition obstruction. The three other parties of the left were clearly disposed to trade their support for the Colau administration in return for agreement on certain specific demands; these did not involve BComú concessions, being largely a question of the prioritization of items on the government agenda. Even the CUP based its demands on items that featured in the Comuns' electoral programme. The year following BComú's election thus saw a lot of negotiation, especially around financial priorities, and seemed to indicate gradual progress towards the creation of a coalition.

From the outset, Colau's team was keen to modify the budget inherited from Trias and to mobilize additional financial resources in order to increase spending on social policy and start using investments to reduce the disparities between the richer and poorer *barrios* of the city. Ultimately it hoped to secure majority support for a new budget, but in the meantime used the raising of credit levels by €100 million (in view of the healthy budget surplus it had inherited) and modifications to the tax ordinances in order to pursue objectives. Colau had support from all parties of the left for these measures and agreed to some specific demands in return, for example, ERC's proposal to extend exemptions from public transport fares to under-16s. Budget negotiations, however, proved more daunting and the initial proposal by the Comuns had to be withdrawn before it reached plenary level, given a general lack of support from other parties. It was only after the Catalan and general elections in September and December 2015 that an improved environment for taking major decisions prevailed.

The early setbacks over finances obliged the administration to carry forward the existing budget. This would have implied cutting anticipated investments and current spending levels, with adverse consequences for social services and social housing, but this was avoided by BComú negotiating support for a budget modification, again raising credit levels, allowing the budget for 2016 to grow by €275 million. Here, the Comuns initially set out to win support from the left and, if possible, secure the abstention of Cs, but the negotiations were complicated by the existence of parallel coalition talks with the Socialists. Although the latter were prospering by March 2016, their likely outcome made it more difficult to bring ERC and the CUP on board for the budget modifications. It took no less than six months of negotiations before the budget changes were finally approved in May, with support from ERC and the PSC, CUP abstention and votes against by CiU, the PSC, PP and Cs.

The key development insofar as inter-party dynamics were concerned was the agreement establishing a provisional stability pact with the Socialists, leading to the formation of a coalition government in May. For the Comuns, this was perceived as a high point, raising their hopes of creating 'a broad front of the left' within the city council. The pact was endorsed by both parties through Internet-based consultations of their members, although with higher levels of participation and endorsement in the PSC than in Barcelona en Comú. There was certainly some opposition to this move within BComú, which earlier had dismissed the Socialists as part of the 'old Barcelona': only 27.6 per cent of the former's 9,422 registered supporters took part in their consultation and the 62.5 per cent level of support for the coalition was offset by a significant negative vote of 32.8 per cent. Arithmetically, this was only a step towards a potential majority on the Council, one which the CUP warned would weaken the administration actually since it would alienate ERC and themselves (Rovira interview, 9 November 2016). In fact, this moment of optimism for the Colau administration quickly passed as it encountered renewed difficulties in gaining additional party support for their road map for the remaining term of office in the form of a new Municipal Action Plan, initially presented by BComú in January 2016.

The coalition with the Socialists was justified by Comuns' leaders by reference to Collboni's public acceptance of the need for political regeneration in the city, which implied tacit self-criticism of the PSC's record in municipal governance up to 2011. It brought some additional personnel to share the tasks of office and district representation and did not involve major policy concessions. For their part, the Socialists managed to raise their profile through Collboni becoming a fifth deputy mayor, with responsibility primarily for culture, but he did not secure the key economy portfolio that he had sought (which remained with Pisarello) and the other three PSC councillors gained only partial responsibility for areas of policy. The entry of the Socialists into a government already formed by a significantly larger, coherent BComú team was to have some impact on cultural policy, involving more contact with conventional as opposed to alternative actors, and in relations with the business community, but essentially the PSC accepted that the Comuns had a mandate for their programme and would lead politically (Salado interview, 1 November 2016; Cid interview, 9 November 2016; Pedret interview, 10 November 2016; Gomà interview, 11 November 2016).

The Socialists were the most amenable of the potential partners of the Comuns. Beyond BComú ideological continuities with the old Maragallist current of the PSC, the Socialists were the keenest to return to office, even in a subordinate position, because of their party's serious electoral decline since 2008. They shared with the Comuns an interest in reforming Spain's unitary constitution, although their views involved a stronger federalist as opposed to confederal emphasis. While the PSOE at this time was opposed to collaboration with Podemos except in exceptional circumstances, the PSC was officially autonomous in matters of alliances and leader Miquel Iceta was favourable to a modified version of the 2003–2010 *tripartito* based on the Comuns, Socialists and ERC. The Socialists, with their relatively market-friendly policies, were wary of some aspects of the Comuns' plans to curb the further development of mass tourism and sceptical of their ideas to develop the cooperative sector of the economy but, rather than voice major political differences, they made unproblematic demands, such as higher spending on job creation and greater investment at *barrio* level.

Some of the demands put forward by Esquerra were equally unproblematic for BComú, such as investment in an extension of the metro network to the city's Zona Franca and the transfer there of the Modelo young offenders' prison. The council decided to sell the old site to finance the construction of a new prison by the regional government and to use the old location to build apartments. ERC appreciated the fact that the Colau administration had reached an agreement with the Generalitat, governed by pro-independence parties. However, it remained opposed to any coalition involving the Socialists and its alliance decisions were now being shaped critically by the independence process and considerations of impact at the Catalan level of governance; this limited its range of potential partners effectively to forces that either backed independence or at least supported a referendum in both words and deeds. Esquerra's municipal leader Alfred Bosch gave as one reason for lending support to the Colau administration in 2015 the fact that she had decided to take part in the *Diada* demonstration on 11 September. He was disappointed, however, by the Comuns' refusal to support Barcelona's affiliation to the Association of Pro-Independence Municipalities (AMI). They abstained in a vote on the issue in September 2015, depriving ERC of the majority needed for its proposal to succeed. BComú criticized a lack of social commitment and a claim to national cultural superiority in the AMI statutes, but also germane to its abstention were internal differences of opinion over the affiliation issue, which left support for a 'right to decide' the only viable compromise that might avoid alienating one sector or another. Yet what was seen by the Comuns as an eminently democratic approach to the national question, reflecting the pluralism of Catalan public opinion, was seen by independence parties as vague and ambiguous. They observed how Colau's expressed willingness to submit the issue of AMI affiliation to public consultation did not materialize.

Over the independence process, the behaviour of the municipal party groups was very much influenced by inter-party dynamics at the regional level. As Chapter 6 will discuss, 'Catalonia, Yes We Can!" (CSQP, Catalunya Sí que es Pot), an alliance formed by ICV-EUiA, Podem and Equo, partly replicating BComú but never embraced by the Comuns, had gained representation in the Catalan Parliament in the September 2015 election and its opposition to the process ensured that it enjoyed quite frosty relations with Esquerra at this more critical level of government for deciding the outcome of the independence initiative. Bosch, formerly ERC leader in the Congress of Deputies, viewed the different levels of government all as part of a single political battle, as a game involving reciprocal collaboration between allies to be conducted at all levels, whereas the Comuns saw themselves as a radical municipalist movement, anxious to concentrate on the changes it had proposed to the electorate. Their desire to 'construct forms of collective identity and citizenship based on residence and participation' did imply a progression from small local victories to interventions at other political levels and the eventual construction of a global alternative (Shea Baird, 2017), but did not regard an independent Catalonia as a necessary step on this road.

The vote on AMI affiliation led ERC to ostentatiously withdraw its confidence in the administration. Even so, its relations with the Comuns in Barcelona remained relatively constructive and conciliatory until the coalition negotiations between BComú and the PSC started to reach fruition. In contrast, the CUP's disposition towards the Colau government was much more demanding from the start and tended to be more so as time passed. The anti-capitalists ruled out government participation from day one. They saw their role on the city council as being subordinate to a class struggle from below that was being waged primarily outside the institutions. In talks on cooperation with the Comuns in June 2015, they opposed the renewal of the city's contract to host the World Mobile Congress, seen as a symbol of global capitalism. While demanding of BComú immediate action on its social promises, their radical 'bottom-up' approach to social transformation made them very sensitive to the Colau administration's handling of public order issues – in particular, its neutrality and patient efforts to mediate during a succession of violent night-time demonstrations and clashes that took place following the eviction of anarchist squatters by the Catalan police (*Mossos d'Esquadra*) from a former bank (the so-called *banco expropiado*) in the district of Gràcia in May 2016. CUP councillor Josep Garganté, who earlier had supported an African street vendor who had been jailed for an attack on a policeman, took an active part in the protests and was among those beaten by the police. While Garganté's sometimes intimidating behaviour drew criticism even from some fellow activists, the CUP urged Colau – with her former history of involvement in the squatters' movement – to condemn 'police brutality'. Instead she called on the Mossos to exercise 'proportionality' when using truncheons and rubber bullets and to focus on protecting the local population from harm.

Nonetheless, the CUP worked with the administration on some social action projects and negotiated with it over policy and financial proposals, showing political acumen by concentrating on items – such as funding for the remunicipalization of service companies – that were common to the BComú and CUP electoral programmes. In March 2016, the CUP backed the administration's enlarged budget proposals but continued to press for further changes as they were processed. Relations suffered both from Ada Colau's attribution of 'pseudo-revolutionary moralism' to the *cupaires* in an interview-based book by a journalist (Serra Carné, 2016) and from BComú's coalition negotiations with the PSC and ERC, seen by the anti-capitalists as evidence of continuity with market-friendly PSC and even CiU policies. What the CUP wanted were *rupturista* actions that denoted a clear break with the existing socio-economic system. Eventually, it facilitated Colau's budget modification in May 2016, but only through abstention, feeling that none of the commitments made by the administration fully incorporated its demands. With BComú proceeding to form their coalition with the Socialists, the CUP warned that in relation to a budget for the following year, it would be demanding the 'whole loaf' rather than the 'crumbs of crumbs' they claimed to have extracted to help the popular classes.

Coalition with the Socialists

The coalition with PSC did not make governance immediately easier, for the Socialists continued to join the opposition parties in pressing for changes to the Comuns' proposed plan (the PEUAT, Plan Especial Urbanístico de Alojamiento, Special Urban Accommodation Plan) for constraints to be placed on the building of new hotels, over which multilateral negotiations were to prolong the task of gaining council approval by over six months. Moreover, in an unprecedented move in October 2016, the opposition parties rejected an initial attempt by the administration to gain approval for the Programme for Municipal Action and new tax ordinances, over which there were contending pressures and incompatible demands from left and right. In fact, although such setbacks contributed to the image of ongoing isolation of the Comuns and institutional weakness, they were not critical to the delivery of the measures, since their contents were provided for by the budget and could be introduced administratively. The previous CiU administration had only managed to get its tax ordinances approved in one year out of four. Parties of the right now began to threaten a vote of no confidence, having been lobbied to do so by business interests (Trias interview, 8 November 2016), but this could not succeed with the PSC on board with BComú, the right divided by electoral rivalry and the Catalan question causing polarization between the parties. It required not simply a majority vote against Colau, but an overall majority in favour of an agreed candidate to replace her as mayor. This provision also meant that on the crucial question of a new budget, the administration had the ultimate advantage of being able to make it a question of confidence if the respective legislation was not approved in the final council plenary of the year: the budget would then become effective if after 30 days the opposition had not succeeded in producing an alternative candidate with majority support. One disadvantage of the municipal context, however, was that the electoral law allowed no possibility of calling early municipal elections, thus denying Colau the option of calling an early election to capitalize on the ongoing popularity of BComú and of herself as mayor, and on public displays of negativity by opposition parties.

The proposed new budget for 2017 was indeed rejected on a 15–26 vote in December 2016, despite some opposition amendments being accepted; but the new year started with greater promise, as the Comuns secured agreements with parties of the left and right during January. ERC support finally allowed the coalition to secure approval of the PEUAT, after the Comuns agreed to reconsider plans affecting three building projects and reassured its PSC partner by making some concessions to the hotelier lobby. Meanwhile broad support was achieved for the administration's housing plan, for which CiU support was negotiated, and the financial basis for tackling inequality over the remaining period in office was created by the procedure of making the new budget, allowing for a rise in social spending of 10.5 per cent, a question of confidence. The larger budget, representing an increase of 4.7 per cent, came into effect in late January 2017 (and it could be rolled forward twice, if the administration so decided). Potentially helping the Comuns too was the decision of Gerard Ardanuy, a member of the CiU group, to break away in April when it was renamed the 'Democrat' group to show its adhesion to the new Catalan European Democratic Party (PDeCAT), representing a refounding of Democratic Convergence of Catalonia. As an independent, there was the possibility that he might be persuaded to vote for some specific coalition measures.

Ada Colau described the final week of January as having been the 'sweetest' week of her administration. It did not, however, set the tone for a whole period of cross-party collaboration in which opposition voting might be limited to a minority. Opposition parties continued to criticize her administration on a range of issues: a council underspend when the accounts for 2016 were published (although caused by factors beyond the administration's control); an alleged promotion of hostility towards the tourist industry; and Colau's response to a metro strike in June. Meanwhile, they resisted the introduction of the Comuns' plan to link up the city's two existing tramlines. What really brought a check to the legislative momentum of the Colau administration, however, was the growing dominance of the independence issue as a key public concern as 2017 progressed. By July, Miquel Iceta was warning that the Socialists would withdraw support for the municipal government if it decided to support the referendum that the pro-independence parties had announced for 1 October.

Polarization over the Catalan issue

During the early 2010s, both the Republican Left and the old Democratic Convergence party had seen their commitment to Catalan sovereignty become radicalized towards explicit advocacy of independence. This had been a gradual process that had accelerated following the Constitutional Court's frustration of Catalan enhanced autonomy hopes in June 2010 and amid pressure from the fast-growing civil society organizations, the ANC (Assemblea Nacional Catalana, Catalan National Assembly) and Òmnium Cultural, which proved able to mobilize Catalans multitudinously on several occasions in the face of intransigence on the part of central government and Spanish policies that emphasized the recentralization of financial control in Madrid in the course of dealing with the sequels to the global financial crisis (Crameri, 2014; 2015; Muro, 2015). Sovereignty-seeking parties had governed Catalonia since 2010 but initially were hampered by the minority status of the first CiU government headed by Mas. After he called early Catalan elections in 2012, however, the pro-sovereignty parties were able to work towards a referendum, thanks to parliamentary collaboration between CiU and ERC over the next three years. A further election in September 2015 then led to the formation of a pro-independence coalition government following the victory of the joint electoral list, JxSí, based on CDC (following the dissolution of CiU in mid-2015), ERC and the Left Movement (MES) (Moviment d'Esquerres), a small party created by former PSC members. With 62 of the 135 seats in the Catalan Parliament, JxSí was eventually able to establish an overall majority through reaching an agreement with the CUP (10 seats) on a pro-independence road map, although CDC was forced to accept the substitution of Mas by Carles Puigdemont, the former mayor of Girona, at the head of the government, to show the radicals that it was now ready to proceed on a unilateral independence course if a final attempt to negotiate with Madrid proved fruitless. After a long history of political dominance in Catalonia via CiU, CDC was fast losing ground by this time, owing both to the adverse publicity brought by financial corruption scandals and to shifts by pro-independence voters towards ERC and the CUP. Attempting to clean up its image and relaunch itself, it held a refoundation congress in June 2016 and eventually took the name of the PDeCAT in September.

From 2016, the government headed by Puigdemont was concentrating all its efforts on implementing the road map for a referendum on independence and was prepared to defy the central government and higher court rulings in the absence of this being facilitated by the Rajoy administration, whose position was that a referendum was impossible under the Spanish Constitution. An illegal consultative referendum, boycotted by opposition parties, had already been held under the second Mas government in November 2014 and had suggested, despite limited participation figures overall, that Barcelona was still a problem for the independence forces, whose support was higher in areas of low population in the interior. Yet the picture was far from static, as seen by the performance of pro-independence parties in the city in the Catalan election of September 2015, in which JxSí and the CUP in aggregate took 47.2 per cent of the vote, compared with 47.7 per cent across the region.

Following their election in Barcelona, the Comuns' position was that although they supported the right to decide and 'the process from below' that was generating Catalan sovereignty demands, they would not endorse the independence plan or indeed any road maps produced by the pro-independence parties, especially the centre-right CiU and its off-spring. BComú's own priority would continue to be the social transformation that inspired its municipal programme. The pro-independence parties meanwhile were encouraged by the results of the September 2015 election and saw their victory as a mandate to proceed, unilaterally if necessary, with their road map. On this occasion, with voters now more polarized over the territorial question, the independence parties finally did well in Barcelona, JxSí taking 37.2 per cent of the votes, some 20 points ahead of second-placed Cs, the main unionist party, on 17.7 per cent, the PSC on 11.5 per cent and the CUP on 10.0 per cent. Particularly worrying for BComú, which as yet lacked a direct political equivalent at the Catalan level, were the poor showing of CSQP, only fifth in the city with 9.8 per cent (fourth with 8.9 per cent across Catalonia) and the victory of Cs in Nou Barris, a district traditionally noted for supporting the left. With the electoral system translating JxSí and CUP votes into an overall majority of the seats in the Catalan Parliament, unilateralist initiatives were soon to move up a gear.

Elections in Catalonia continued to produce widely contrasting results across different levels of government, however, and the Spanish general elections of December 2015 and June 2016 were to involve much stronger left-right competition. In them, En Comú Podem (ECP, In Common We Can), an alliance of the CSQP's components with BComú, proceeded to triumph in Catalonia, partly because the focus was on Spanish governance and thus the efforts by the left to defeat the PP, yet also because the direct involvement of Ada Colau in the campaign, compared with her low profile during the Catalan election campaign, was seen as a game-changer. ECP's position, like that of BComú, was to support a referendum 'with guarantees', meaning that, to be effective, it would need to be agreed upon with central government if possible, be compatible with Spain's legal and constitutional framework, and possess international credibility. Colau redefined her position in January 2017, after Rajoy confirmed his refusal to authorize a referendum; she no longer insisted on its negotiation with central government but reiterated that it would need to be 'effective' and added that the Comuns would want to know the actual question to be posed in the referendum before deciding how to respond to such an event. The difficulty in practice was that not only the Rajoy government but all the major Spanish parties except Podemos viewed any Catalan referendum on independence as being incompatible with the Constitution, which vested sovereignty in the Spanish people. BComú's position still seemed problematic to many Catalans and caused the Comuns some embarrassment on occasions when they were pressed to define themselves immediately on actual pro-independence steps, as opposed to the generic principle of holding a referendum, on which most Catalan democrats were agreed.

The Comuns opposed the unilateralist agenda, yet not to the point of siding with the so-called 'constitutionalist' parties (PP, Cs and PSC) that actively tried to block the process. What many on both sides of the independence issue saw as BComú's ambiguity on the territorial question was partly a result of their need to reconcile independence, federal and confederal preferences within their own ranks. At the same time, their Catalanism and espousal of participative democracy left them fundamentally supportive of a Catalan vote on the issue and made them oppose state attempts to prevent it and show solidarity with *independentista* activists who were penalized for flouting bans and restrictions. In December 2015, a vote in the Presidency committee in the city hall expressed support for a declaration in the Catalan Parliament that had declared a complete 'break' with Catalonia's constitutional status quo; the Comuns abstained in this vote but backed a CiU motion calling for support to be given to other municipalities in the province that were under investigation for passing similar declarations.

For Colau, there were also issues of institutional responsibility to consider as a mayor who had said she would govern for all the citizens of her city. While a majority of the CSQP parliamentary group stayed away from the Diada demonstration in September 2016, owing to their opposition to the unilateralist process, Colau decided to attend, explaining that she felt the mayor should be present at such an important event in the Catalan calendar and wanted to show her opposition to the judicialization of the Catalan question by the Rajoy government. Earlier in the day, she also attended a separate Diada rally organized by ECP in Sant Boi de Llobregat which, under the slogan 'For a Popular Catalanism!', commemorated the first Diada to be tolerated by the authorities following the announcement of a restoration of democracy in 1976. In a newspaper article at this time, Colau maintained that Catalans should be able to vote freely to show whether they preferred federalism, confederalism or independence, and described this as a democratic challenge rather than a challenge to democracy (*El País*, 10 September 2016). Recognition of the pluralism of Catalan opinion was not something that independence parties wanted to hear from her, however; they contended that federalism was less of a real possibility than independence, given the recentralizing trends evident in the Rajoy government's policies.

Barcelona's involvement in the Catalan process grew in February 2017 with the approval of an institutional declaration by the city council in support of the national pact subscribed to the previous December by organizations and institutions supporting a referendum on independence. On this occasion, both BComú and ERC voted for the proposal presented by CiU, while the Socialists joined Cs and the

PP in opposing it. The CUP abstained, since the Puigdemont government was still pressing for an agreement with Madrid on this, which implied operating within the Spanish legal framework, whereas the anti-capitalists advocated disobedience. Further reservations were expressed by Colau, however, in June when the Catalan government announced that it would be holding a referendum on 1 October and the independence parties urged her to use her position as mayor to facilitate this event. BComú was too internally diverse with respect to territorial politics to formulate a common response to the question set by the Catalan authorities for this consultation, 'Do you want Catalonia to become an independent state in the form of a republic?' Notwithstanding their republican sentiments, the Comuns continued to qualify their support by saying the referendum would need to be effective and enjoy international guarantees of recognition. Echoing Podemos, Colau described the referendum as more like a 'mobilization'. Keen to protect municipal employees and the Council from the risk of prosecution, she ruled out the opening of official polling stations, but ultimately, following a meeting with Puigdemont in mid-September, did proceed to facilitate voting in municipal buildings such as civic centres, staffed by volunteers.

The referendum placed further BComú-PSC collaboration in jeopardy, yet the Socialist municipal group initially disagreed with the view of party leader Iceta that facilitation of voting on 1 October would be a breaking point. The coalition lasted into November, but was in deep trouble once the PSOE had joined the PP and Cs in supporting the application of Article 155 of the Constitution to impose direct rule in Catalonia. Following the referendum, on 10 October Puigdemont's government had issued a somewhat confusingly formulated proclamation of a republic, but had temporarily suspended it in the hope of eliciting international mediation. Political polarization now reached a peak as the pro-independence parties accused the PSC of becoming an 'accomplice' of repression and ERC and the PDeCAT offered to support Colau's administration in Barcelona if she would end the coalition with the Socialists. If she did, she would face a return to a smaller minority government and greater reliance on variable geometry; if she did not, she risked obstruction by all the pro-independence parties over every issue. Either way, her administration was likely to emerge weaker.

On 6 October, the city council had approved a motion agreed upon by the pro-independence parties describing the central government's response to the referendum as a 'covert coup d'état' and portraying the outcome of the referendum as a democratic mandate that should be respected. It succeeded with the help of BComú abstention. While regarding the referendum as a legitimate expression of Catalan opinion and condemning the violence used by Spanish police forces in Madrid's operation to prevent voting, some 900 Catalans having been injured, the Comuns were careful to avoid siding with either the pro-independence or the unionist bloc. Both Colau and Collboni rejected UDI and Article 155 as ways forward. Colau spoke of the unionist demonstrations during the month – which the PSC supported – as equally legitimate expressions of Catalan opinion and she told Puigdemont that the results of the referendum did not entitle him to proceed to unilateral independence. The 'yes' vote of 90 per cent in the referendum represented 37.8 per cent of the electoral register and was qualified by a participation rate of 43 per cent, yet in the context of Spanish actions to prevent it, its volume was substantial enough to make a significant impression on international opinion, though not to bring mediation attempts.

Those who found themselves in no man's land in the conflict, as the Comuns did now, were to become little more than spectators on 27 October as the Catalan Parliament approved the proposal of the independence parties to declare independence and commence a process leading to the constitution of a republic; the Spanish Senate responded with immediate imposition of Article 155, after which the Madrid government deposed the Catalan government and called a Catalan election, to be held on 21 December. This in no way resolved the battle over the future of Catalonia, however. Unionist hopes that the pro-independence camp would become leaderless as a result of state intervention were dashed, partly because of the stratagem of Puigdemont and other members of the deposed Catalan government who travelled to Brussels at the end of October to avoid detention and prosecution. In December, the pro-independence forces would go on to confirm their majority status in the Catalan Parliament, although now they were divided organizationally between a new Junts per Catalunya (JxCat) list reflecting Puigdemont's own enhanced personal influence (at the expense of PDeCAT), one headed by ERC and the CUP. None of them secured as many seats as Cs (36), which became the main standard bearer of unionism, but together JxCat (34), ERC (32) and the CUP (4) now had a total of 70 seats in Parliament, although some of its members were now in exile, facing extradition proceedings or in prison, awaiting trial, and thus the potential voting majority of the independence parties was now in question.

The Comuns isolated

For the municipal coalition in Barcelona, the writing was on the wall by late October when the opposition parties all voted against a new set of tax ordinances. By now opposition behaviour was overwhelmingly influenced by the wider Catalan situation and the coalition soon fell victim to it. An attempt by the Socialist municipal group to present a resolution dissociating itself both from the use of Article 155 and UDI was thwarted by the independence parties, who managed to restrict city council debate in late October to just the suspension of autonomy. The Comuns and Socialists thus ended up on different sides when it came to voting on a PDeCAT-ERC motion supporting Catalonia's institutions, rejecting the application of Article 155 and condemning the jailing of the leaders of the ANC and Òmnium Cultural, Jordi Sànchez and Jordi Cuixart. BComú voted for the motion while the Socialists voted against. The tipping point for the coalition came on 3 November when eight members of the former Puigdemont government, including deputy prime minister and ERC president Oriol Junqueras, were remanded in custody in prison, pending prosecution over the declaration of independence. Although deeply critical of the Catalan government's unilateralism, Colau and the Comuns continued to regard the deposed government as legitimate and deplored the Rajoy government's policy of prosecuting the leading political figures of the independence movement; the trials of those jailed would not begin until February 2019. The use of preventive imprisonment produced universal condemnation within BComú and a groundswell of demands that the Socialists be expelled from the government for supporting Article 155. A BComú plenary voted by 90 per cent in favour of a digital consultation of the Comuns' 10,000 registered supporters, of whom 54.2 per cent voted to end the coalition. Gerardo Pisarello commented that if the PSC had held an internal consultation on the imposition of Article 155, the BComú consultation would not have been necessary. Colau, who had defended the collaboration with the Socialists up until the plenary and had a good working relationship with Collboni, proceeded to end the coalition, saying that the PSC had moved to the right by endorsing the PSOE's solidarity with Rajoy over the Catalan issue and claiming that Iceta had exemplified it by taking 'selfies' with Catalan PP leaders at a unionist demonstration in late October.

Adding to the image of isolation of the Comuns in the city was a disappointing first outing for the successor to CSQP, 'Catalunya en Comú-Podem' (CatComú-Podem), in the Catalan elections in December, which against the backcloth of the prosecution of people deemed responsible for the October challenge was characterized by strong polarization of the votes, based on the territorial conflict. Whereas CSQP had been predicted to win 12–14 of the 135 seats in a recent CEO poll, the new CatComú-Podem won only 8 seats, compared with the 11 won by CSQP in 2015 and 13 won by ICV-EUiA in 2012. Collective success for the pro-independence parties in this election and individual success for Cs (36 seats compared with just 4 for the PP) affected the relationship between the mainstream independence parties and the Comuns: whereas beforehand the former had tried to court the latter with a view to occupying the centre ground and isolating the PP, now the independence parties felt more confident about winning in Barcelona and thus became more competitive in relation both to the Comuns and Cs.

Unionist parties meanwhile regarded the Comuns as having shifted closer to the independence camp and cited as evidence Colau's reception of the families of the imprisoned political leaders, her decision not to take part in an official reception for King Felipe VI at the World Mobile Congress in February 2018 because of his chastisement of Catalan leaders and failure to mention the police violence, and her participation in a demonstration against the use of preventive imprisonment. In fact, the Comuns' position on the territorial question itself remained unchanged: their outspokenness over central government policy at this time emanated rather from concerns that democracy was being undermined by the judicialization of policy in response to the Catalan challenge, not only through the use of preventive imprisonment (supposedly to prevent those facing charges going into exile abroad), but also by resorting to charges such as sedition and rebellion that carried very long prison sentences.

All-round opposition hostility towards the Comuns had thus become a defining feature of municipal politics in Barcelona by 2018, causing Colau in early February to comment that the municipal election campaign had started, almost a year and a half before the event itself. At this point, every one of the 30 opposition councillors expressed opposition to the governing party's budget proposals. Nonetheless, BComú was able to get its budget for the year adopted by again posing a question of confidence and thereby exploiting the disunity of the opposition. The new budget provided for increases in social spending, investment and the human resources of the council. Thus, the Comuns were able to continue to implement existing items of council policy, yet they now found it exceedingly difficult to negotiate support for new measures, notably their high-profile tram connection project. Although the Socialists were in favour of it, ERC, which had favoured the idea in its election manifesto, refused to do so, despite being offered concessions in respect of the details of the scheme. By March, the Left Republicans had established a small lead over BComú in opinion polls and, on top of fundamental disagreements over the Catalan 'process', this proved harmful to constructive ERC-BComú relations. Bosch, as the candidate expected to stand again in the forthcoming municipal election, opined in a newspaper interview that little had changed in Barcelona since 2015 and presented Colau herself as responsible (*El País*, 21 March 2018).

The administration was obliged to shelve its largest single urban planning project, namely, the tram link, only to face a further rebuff in April over its public participation plans. These had centred upon the idea of introducing regular opportunities for citizens to propose and vote on popular initiatives; the latter would be combined in a single annual digital consultation, a *multiconsulta*, for which proposals needed a minimum of 15,000 signatures. Opposition from the other party groups led the administration to concentrate finally in 2018 just on the issue that had attracted most public support: the remunicipalization of water. This episode showed just how implacable the opposition parties were, for some that had supported the principle of policy participation earlier opposed the Comuns' consultation proposals now, even though the regulations authorized Council members to vote to block them only if the plans were legally problematic – not because of the substance of the proposed policy change. Defeated in a plenary session in April, BComú would eventually get its *multiconsulta* approved in October – too late for the first consultation to be held ahead of the municipal election.

In the case of other left-wing parties, frustrating the consultation plan risked upsetting some of their own supporters, as did the earlier issue of the tram link, given majority support for it in public opinion polls. The CUP, which voted against the consultation on the grounds that it was unnecessary since there was already an electoral mandate for remunicipalization, went on to rectify its position following dissent within its ranks. Meanwhile, both left and right began to attack the administration over an alleged deterioration in public safety in the Ciutat Vella district by forcing the holding of an extraordinary council session to discuss issues such as encampments temporarily established by homeless people and sympathetic NGO activists in Plaça de Catalunya and the presence of *narcopisos* in the *barrio* of Raval, these being empty apartments in dilapidated buildings, used by criminals as bases for selling drugs.

Would this crescendo of condemnation from opposition parties, not to mention powerful private sector lobbies within the city, prove electorally damaging to the Comuns? A year ahead of elections, BComú was politically isolated and appeared weak and more vulnerable to challengers in the independence camp, especially if the mainstream forces could unite to form a unitary pro-independence electoral list. Public opinion polls showed some deterioration in the Comuns' standing, although not a critical one in the still fragmented but evolving context of political competition in Barcelona. During the first two years of their term in office, the Colau administration had enjoyed quite comfortable approval ratings: among them 67.1 per cent in the municipal poll of June 2017, with BComú leading also in terms of voting intentions, although facing a growing challenge from ERC, with Bosch enjoying a marginally higher personal rating than Colau. Notwithstanding the defeats and setbacks inflicted by the opposition in the Spring of 2018, by the end of three years in government, the erosion in BComú support was significant yet not necessarily game-changing. For the first time, those approving of the mayor's record (44.8 per cent) were fewer than those who felt she was not doing well (48.6 per cent). However, a projection at this point had the Comuns still leading with 9–10 seats, followed by ERC and Cs on 8–9, PDeCAT 6, PSC 5, CUP 4 and PP 0 (GESOP poll, *El Periódico*, 21 May 2018).

BComú's ability to overcome obstruction by opposition parties was greatly limited, yet even now there were occasional opportunities to introduce further measures in the city and the possibility of changes in the Catalan and Spanish contexts that might mitigate its minority institutional situation. Public pressure over the housing crisis, for instance, made it harder for the left-wing electoral rivals of the Comuns to opt for an endless spoiling strategy in relation to new BComú measures to increase the stock of social housing. In June 2018, ERC, the PSC and the CUP voted together with the Comuns at committee stage on proposals requiring builders to devote 30 per cent of new apartment builds and refurbishments to social housing, while PDeCAT and Cs abstained. The possibility of changes in the wider environment was signalled by two developments: growing post-referendum divergence among the pro-independence forces, with many ERC and PDeCAT members favouring some measure of retrenchment and seeing a need to build bridges with the Comuns; and by the more dramatic change of government in Spain following a successful vote of no confidence presented by the PSOE against Rajoy in May 2018, following the devastating impact on the PP of a Supreme Court verdict in the Gürtel financial corruption case. This enabled Pedro Sánchez of the PSOE to form a new government.

For the Comuns, there was relatively little they could do about the wider political environment that would frame the May 2019 municipal election, although they clearly wished it would have a left-right municipal character rather than be dominated by the issue of independence. Nor did they have any control over the efforts by Puigdemont supporters to negotiate a unitary electoral list with the PDeCAT and ERC, which proved only partially successful. They could still use their fourth year in government to implement the contents of the municipal action plan as much as possible. Their challenges were to do enough to convince voters that a process of social change had commenced, to put across to the electorate exactly what the administration had been able to deliver and to remobilize their own activists and supporters for what promised to be a very tight electoral contest.

5 The Comuns in office
Achievements and shortcomings

Assessing the degree of change that BComú was able to introduce or promote during four years in office is bound to be a somewhat provisional exercise if attempted immediately afterwards. The crucial issue of consolidation depended both on the outcome of the 2019 municipal election in Barcelona and on future political developments both there and beyond. Nevertheless, 'end-of-term' analysis is relevant, not least because impressions of performance by the Colau administration informed the behaviour of voters and of future potential coalition partners. Without aiming to be exhaustive, this chapter aims to discuss the achievements and limitations of the Comuns in office in 2015–2019 by reference to political culture, economic management, services, housing, feminization and rights, the environment, tourism, global outreach and security challenges.

To attempt a fair appraisal, one must be wary of the approach used by rival parties at election time, according to which any shortfalls in the achievement of electoral pledges provide cumulative evidence of political failure. While attainment of targets is certainly an important indicator of performance, one needs to begin by recognizing the institutional constraints upon municipal governments in Spain. Municipalities are primarily tasked with the provision of services, whose range varies according to size of population. Where populations exceed 50,000, for example, these extend to transport and environmental protection. In the case of Barcelona, some key services, including transport, are managed at the metropolitan level. A lot of crucial policy competences for matters germane to social transformation and particularly to security, however, are held by central or regional government or subject to joint jurisdictions. Efforts by the Comuns to implement their programme thus relied on policy initiatives finding some degree of complementary action by higher levels of government and neither in Spain (until June 2018 with the switch from the PP

(Partido Popular, People's Party) to a PSOE (Partido Socialista Obrero Español, Spanish Socialist Workers' Party) government) nor in Catalonia was there a left-of-centre party in office during this period.

Even if the Comuns had coincided more with left-leaning administrations at other governmental levels, there was still the difficulty that major powers over issues such as health, education and policing were vested in a Generalitat that at this time was much more financially constrained than Barcelona. Even when, during Puigdemont's government, Colau was able to reach agreement with him on some projects, the city had to produce a disproportionate share of the funding. It devoted significantly more resources than the Catalan government to tackling the housing crisis, despite the competence being vested primarily at regional level. This situation was unsustainable in the longer term. By July 2018, the Colau administration was demanding €350 million from the Generalitat in respect of shortfalls in Catalan investment in services, such as nurseries and housing since 2012. In the aftermath of a financial crisis and deep recession, the city was being seriously underfunded by both Spain and Catalonia (and the latter by the Spanish state).

Far from believing in 'socialism in one city', the Comuns had a pragmatic, positive attitude towards inter-institutional cooperation. They presented specific proposals, sought negotiations around them and attempted to generate pressure by lobbying together with any allies if they were being ignored by other governments, as invariably they were by Rajoy. In other words, if the division of institutional competences was an obstacle, the Comuns did not trim their ambitions and settle for what could be done autonomously at municipal level: rather, they strove to make people more aware of the division of institutional competences and agitated for municipal powers (especially for major cities) to be enhanced, while also developing a political strategy aimed at intervening more influentially at higher levels of governance in the future.

The institutional configuration of competences proved especially limiting for BComú's efforts to address the housing crisis, which worsened at a pace that could not be countered simply through a municipal response. A rising number of home evictions, often related to a desire by owners to convert residential property into tourist apartments, was increasingly triggered by the inability to afford higher rents rather than mortgage repayment difficulties. Rent rises had been regulated more liberally under the Urban Rentals Law (LAU) of 2013, making investment in rental properties more profitable, especially with a view to the tourist market. Under the LAU, most tenancy agreements lasted only three years, after which tenants often were forced to leave their homes by the size of rent rises, the average rent in Barcelona reaching €900 monthly by 2018. It was not until May 2019 that the Generalitat attempted to regulate abusive rent increases and to concede to Barcelona the power to do likewise in particularly problematic localities.

The lack of institutional cooperation was evident also in the shared responsibility area of environmental pollution, despite strong European pressure on Spain to act to reduce pollution from cars, which was at critical levels in Madrid and Barcelona. While within Catalonia disagreement between the Generalitat, the AMB (Àrea Metropolitana de Barcelona (Metropolitan Area of Barcelona) and Barcelona eventually led the city to proceed unilaterally with car restrictions, in February 2018 Spanish PP environment minister Isabel García Tejerina disowned the problem, claiming that pollution was a responsibility for each town hall to deal with.

With the change of Spanish government in 2018, there was finally the prospect of new state measures to give more security to tenants and prevent the abusive rent increases. The Sánchez government also offered intelligence support from the National Police to help deal with the problem of empty tourist apartments being used by criminal networks as bases for selling drugs; and it took steps to withdraw PP government appeals to the courts which had effectively suspended Catalan laws on energy poverty and evictions.

In relations with the Catalan government, meanwhile, there was a distinct lack of empathy between Mas and Colau, the latter being unwilling to ignore the Generalitat's debts to the municipality (as Trias had done). There was tension over the ending of the city's subsidy of the Spanish Formula 1 Grand Prix. Colau's relations with Puigdemont were better, leading to agreements on various city projects, partial recognition of the debt and the use of municipal buildings for voting in the referendum. This collaboration was halted by the imposition of direct rule from October 2017 until June 2018, after which relations resumed on a much stiffer note under Puigdemont's successor, Quim Torra. Colau's administration managed to persuade the Generalitat to pass on an increased proportion of the tourist tax revenue collected in Barcelona, which rose from 33 per cent to 50 per cent, but it did not get the 100 per cent it called for on the grounds that the city produced half the region's income from the tax.

One must also note that the Comuns themselves saw the pursuit of goals as relying on a degree of 'partnership' between the administration and the activities of like-minded citizens. While the Comuns have been criticized by the far left for perceiving 'institutions as the main instrument through which to implement change' (Stobart, 2018) – and in office exhibited strong tendencies in this direction – their praxis reveals a view of social transformation as not simply a matter of governmental action but also of initiatives by organized groups within communities, for example, through the green energy cooperative, Som Energia, created several years before the launch of Guanyem Barcelona. BComú's activism at the societal level was greatly weakened by the entry of prominent social activists into government from 2015 and by the diversion of effort into the political attempt to build a left-wing confluence at the Catalan level. Nonetheless, it would be unfair to conclude that the Comuns have been guilty as charged, of institutionalism, to the extent that parties such as the PSC and ICV had traditionally been.

Alert to the risks of becoming 'institutionalized' within the existing system and losing their radical edge thereby, the Comuns took steps to counter them. Ongoing activist methods continued to be used when institutional means to achieve political objectives proved ineffectual. When efforts to prevent housing repossessions failed through persuasion or legal action, Gala Pin (a key member of the Colau administration responsible for the Ciutat Vella district) appealed to activists through Twitter to stage demonstrations to thwart evictions. On various occasions, BComú leaders including Colau herself joined public demonstrations aimed at influencing other institutional actors, as in February 2017 during a march by 160,000 people calling on the Spanish government to fulfil its obligations to refugees and in April 2018 in a massive protest over the imprisonment of pro-independence leaders following the Catalan referendum. Moreover, the Comuns remained committed to open government and participation by citizens although failing to gain council approval for an initial *multiconsulta* to be held in 2018. Finally, they took steps to boost the resource base of NGOs working for similar policy goals to their own, by substantially increasing municipal subsidies to them, prompting opposition outcries about 'favouritism'.

Addressing the political culture

The lack of ideological zeal of the Comuns should not be allowed to obscure the fact that they aspired to a far-reaching transformation of the political culture. They were to challenge the dominant cultures informing political life, aiming to see progressive left-wing and liberal ideas become hegemonic in society in the long term. This activity involved symbolic rejections of Spain's authoritarian past, hierarchical structures and patriarchal traditions, as well as a questioning of the nationalist centre-right outlook associated with years of CiU (Convergència i Unió, Convergence and Unity) dominance in Catalonia.

These 'rejections' were accompanied by active measures to promote greater participation by citizens in city governance, breaking with established forms of elitist and often corrupt politics.

The Comuns demonstrated more radicalism than the Socialists in rejecting the historical compromises that the traditional left had entered into with conservative forces during the Spanish transition to democracy. BComú saw the constant repudiation of monarchist and other Spanish establishment figures as practised by the CUP (Candidatura d'Unitat Popular, Popular Unity Candidature) as counter-productive, making it harder to reach out to those who respected them; Colau's behaviour in dealings with other office holders tended to be 'correct', except when there was particularly strong questioning of them in society – as when she boycotted the receptions for King Felipe VI at the World Mobile Congress in Barcelona in 2018 and 2019 following his endorsement of the methods used by Rajoy's government in the attempt to thwart the independence referendum. Symbolically, however, under pressure from the CUP, the Comuns did break with tradition by removing monarchist iconography such as portraits of the King from city hall, seeing it as contradicting the republican traditions of Barcelona; and they also repudiated authoritarian and colonial legacies by having plazas renamed, for example, the Plaza de la Hispanidad with the name of Pablo Neruda. Equally, the cultural domain was viewed as an arena in which to break with Catalan nationalist versions of history as a long saga of confrontation between Catalonia and Spain, to address the grim realities of the Francoist past and to promote awareness of human rights issues. The Born Cultural Centre was changed dramatically under their influence. No longer primarily a monument to the events surrounding the siege of Barcelona in 1714, the centre began to focus on a range of more contemporary themes and to reflect diversity in the traditions of the city, starting with an exhibition that challenged the myths of Francoism and raised questions about justice for its victims. Cultural policy more generally tended to support public rather than private museums.

Meanwhile, at the directly political level, actions to combat elitism and corruption in government were complemented by steps to increase the influence of citizens in decision-making and to reduce hierarchy. In their immediate environment, the Comuns gave a say to anyone who registered their political support online (i.e., their *inscritos*) in decisions on major issues, such as coalition formation, and they sought to find ways to involve the whole electorate on a regular basis. Consultations over the new Municipal Action Plan were opened to the public and some 39,000 people took part in the drafting process – a moderate achievement, given that 170,000 people had voted for BComú in the election. Another initiative was to lower the level of support required for municipal citizen initiatives to go forward, from 1 per cent of the 1.1 million voters on the municipal register to 15,000, and to remove the 50 per cent threshold for a vote on a proposal to be deemed valid. Though the staging of the *multiconsulta* was blocked by the opposition and thus the proposed remunicipalization of water was not voted on, despite having attracted 28,700 signatures, the enabling regulations were approved in October 2018, providing for consultations every year except in local election years. The only previous municipal consultation had been held on an ad hoc basis, in 2010.

In addition to their code of ethics, under which BComú councillors, mayors and aides took only €2,200 a month in salary and expenses and channelled the rest to fund social projects, municipal salaries in general were reduced by 22–24 per cent and a new city code of conduct was drawn up; this regulated the behaviour of several hundred elected officials, directors and aides, forbidding them from moving directly to or from the private sector and requiring them to return any gifts worth €50 or more. The Comuns also established an electronic letterbox through which citizens could make allegations about unethical behaviour by municipal staff or in entities or companies working with the Council, to be investigated by a new Transparency and Good Practice Office within six months. They also publicized all aspects of council finances, in the name of transparency. Their desire to differentiate their politics from the corruption-tainted traditions of established parties, and to make better, more accountable use of public finances, also led to the city officially taking part in trial proceedings against former CiU figures accused of political corruption offences.

Arguably, the moral high ground occupied by BComú was as important to their retention of public approval, and to Colau's own popularity, as what it could achieve in terms of tangible improvements in people's lives. However, here they sometimes lost face, particularly through not being able to deliver a consultation in 2018. Moreover, creating opportunities for citizens to decide was no guarantee of public satisfaction. When local consultation was used as a response to the Can Vies dispute, it brought evidence of a deep division in public opinion over the future of the building (*El País*, 22 February 2017). Moves to deepen political participation did not change the fact that politics often involves the challenge of taking difficult decisions. The Comuns certainly expanded the range of social groups with which the municipal government interacted (Serra Carné, 2016: 145), but could not please all of them, all of the time, as they were criticized for trying to do by the CUP (Rovira interview, 9 November 2016.).

Finances and the economy

The pursuit of a left agenda aimed at shifting the balance of forces between political representatives and economic actors, reducing social inequality, improving public services and enhancing the rights of disadvantaged groups in society had much in common with social democratic agendas, yet showed greater radicalism in areas such as the economic model and feminization. The financial basis underpinning achievement remained relatively strong compared with that of reforming administrations in other parts of Spain. BComú's management of the public accounts was cautious and transparent, yet it boosted public spending substantially (by almost 10 per cent in 2018 alone), especially social spending, without causing budget deficits. Even in 2018, when the municipal government was hit by a fall in income from property transaction taxes, the administration remained solvent and cuts in overall investment proved unnecessary. That summer, Colau was able to claim that hers was the city within Spain that was investing most in social spending (€850 million), especially in poorer districts. A campaign against tax fraud, involving increased levels of inspection, publicized the names of those owing more than €1 million in tax, concentrated on the largest companies and collected €69 million in fines.

There were some innovative economic measures, particularly a new local currency piloted in 10 poor *barrios* along the River Besós from October 2018. Operating through a mobile app, this was the 'citizens economic resource' (REC), of equal value to the euro. By this time, some 1,000 low-income families, already on social benefits, had begun to receive a so-called municipal income (B-Mincome) through an EU-funded project, on condition that they used one-quarter of this aid in the new currency on purchases from some 70 local retailers who subscribed to the project, seeing it as a possible lifeline following successive shop closures in the area. The objective of the Comuns was to enhance social inclusion, help SMEs and inject funds into the social economy, which overall represented 8 per cent of employment in Barcelona. Colau justified the priority afforded to SMEs by pointing out that 95 per cent of companies in the city employed less than 10 people. There was some PSC (Partit dels Socialistes de Catalunya, Socialist Party of Catalonia) criticism of the scheme for potentially fuelling a dependency culture, but this was mild compared with the constant opposition to BComú policy that came from powerful economic sectors in the city, which campaigned incessantly against the remunicipalization of services and the controls on tourist expansion.

Despite the prioritization here of SMEs, many of the complaints about BComú policy came from owners of small bars and restaurants, affected by restrictions on the tabled terrace areas adjacent to their premises and the municipal charges for such concessions, or shopkeepers who felt they were losing trade to illegal street vendors. However, it was the multinationals that possessed the real wherewithal to contest municipal measures in the courts and at least delay their impact. Under the Comuns, there was less overt city hall courtship of multinationals than there had been in the past, yet with unemployment figures falling only slowly from 11.16 per cent in 2015 (http://datosmacro.expansion.com), there was still a considerable municipal effort made to attract new foreign investment that would generate jobs and to safeguard the income associated with hosting the World Mobile Congress and other international events. Nonetheless, the Comuns' sympathies were evident during various industrial disputes in which they showed support for the workers and they also used council contracts as a means of insisting on new ethical standards within companies with which the city council worked. Colau expressed interest in working with multinationals to increase their contribution to the city community but, given their tendency to export their profits elsewhere, she never saw this as a priority.

Business representatives were critical of council efforts to reverse the trend towards privatization. In part, ideologically-driven, BComú's policy of remunicipalizing some services and municipalizing others was also a reaction against recent pro-market policies that had brought job losses. Municipalization began modestly with nurseries that had been part-privatized by Trias and it continued with women's support services and Barcelona's television company. Then came some major battles against big firms that had been providing electricity to the city and water to the metropolitan area. Both steps needed full council approval and following that quickly became subject to protracted court proceedings initiated by existing providers. Policy here was informed by the administration's desire to control essential services and expand the council's workforce by 10 per cent, from 12,000 people. Behind all this was an underlying challenge to the economic model of the city based on public-private partnership, aiming to replace it with municipal economic leadership and support for cooperatives, in the belief that the economy could be made more accountable and serve public interests better.

Services

There were some areas where municipalization was considered but in the end discarded as either uneconomical, too complex to take on, or politically impossible for lack of cross-party support. These included a funeral service (although the administration did manage to negotiate a cheaper funeral scheme with existing providers); waste collection and disposal services; and the provision of day care, where externalization could not be ended, as promised in the electoral programme, owing to the legal framework.

Municipalization made its biggest mark in the field of energy provision. Adding to BComú's determination here was the refusal of existing providers – Gas Natural and the electricity company Endesa (along with the water provider Agbar) – to do more to help people living below the poverty line. The Colau administration fined companies for cutting off energy supplies to the poor for non-payment of bills without adequate notification. It urged the energy companies to go beyond existing schemes based on social bonds and to assume at least half the cost of maintaining supplies to debtors out of profits. Early on, the Comuns required new buildings to have thermal solar panels to heat water and invested in the installation of panels on municipal buildings; later they created Barcelona Energia as a municipal company to buy and sell electricity to power municipal buildings and street lighting from July 2018 and to generate surplus energy for domestic use. Done in the name of producing a fairer, more efficient and sustainable energy market that would allow the city hall to free itself of reliance on an electricity oligopoly and reduce its energy bills, the Colau administration initially attracted criticism from ecology groups for looking to use incineration plants as well as photovoltaic panels and a biomass plant to source Barcelona Energia, until a rethink led to the use of energy that was green as well as renewable.

The main opposition came from big energy companies, worried about the precedent that Barcelona Energia, the largest entirely public power distributor in Spain, was setting for other municipalities, not least in the metropolitan area. In 2017, they hit back by refusing to tender for new supply contracts containing social clauses, which were needed until the new municipal provider could replace them; they also took their complaints to a court that forced the administration to suspend the tendering process, whereby smaller companies had hoped to benefit. The following year, however, Barcelona Energia was up and running, making the city self-sufficient in energy and able to provide electricity for some 20,000 homes, although prevented by competition law from growing further.

Other municipal initiatives ran into greater obstacles. The battle over the remunicipalization of water, for which BComú secured city council support in 2016, proved more protracted once it reached the courts. In the field of transportation, meanwhile, the Comuns' flagship tram project was eventually blocked both by local and Catalan political opposition, this being a decision needing city-metropolitan-regional agreement. Barcelona thus remained with two stretches of tramline linking the central Eixample district with the outlying Besós and Llobregat areas, but no connection between them. In contrast, the BComú administration brought significant extensions to the metro network and a threefold expansion of the bicycle lane network, which came to account for 2.5 per cent of city travel (up from 2 per cent), compared with public transport, 40 per cent, cars, 26 per cent and walking, 32 per cent. These lanes remained narrow, however, and were, along with a widespread failure to use helmets and the use of earphones, a factor in the rising number of bicycle accidents. Telecommunications, meanwhile, saw continuity with existing providers, once Vodaphone and Telefónica had agreed to accept new contracts that embodied recent collective agreements with their workers.

In relation to social services, the municipal administration was severely hampered by the division of competences and frequently bemoaned a lack of support from the Generalitat. Apart from lacking funds, the latter maintained a traditional welfare approach whereas under deputy mayor Laia Ortiz, the Comuns tried to shift the emphasis from benefits to rights and pursued the ideal of social equality, yet found this very complicated in practice, partly owing to the very limited tax information available to them. BComú expanded the municipal staffing of social services, achieving a higher rate of responsiveness to the public and introduced progressively-rated tariffs in nurseries. It established a new municipal dental service, to provide complementary care for benefits recipients reliant on the public health system.

It may have been too much to expect a reduction in social inequality in just four years, largely through municipal efforts. Municipal data on family income suggest that the Comuns' prioritization of spending in the poorer *barrios*, along with rising employment levels by 2017, did bring a small decrease in inequality between the richest and poorest *barrios*, but income remained below average in some two-thirds of them (*El País*, 9 January 2017, 8 January 2018, 29 January 2018).

Housing

Public provision of accommodation had been so neglected by government in recent decades that by 2015 housing was deemed to be quite marginal to the concept of services. Responding to problems that would continue to grow following their election to office – through fast rising rents and a Constitutional Court suspension of the Catalan anti-eviction law of 2015, lasting until 2019 – the Comuns made this a key priority. They tackled it through a series of emergency measures, attempts to work with existing private owners of (sometimes empty) properties that might be brought into the social housing sector, the building of new rented accommodation and lobbying for higher-level governments to collaborate more in addressing the accommodation crisis. The latter was marked by rent rises in the city of 28 per cent in 2014–2018, occupations of properties by families no longer able to afford their mortgages or rents (especially in Nou Barris), repossessions (by this time primarily concentrated in the rental sector), tenants obliged to leave their neighbourhood to find accessible accommodation elsewhere, and growing homelessness. The crisis affected people from the middle class as well as humbler backgrounds and, in conjunction with high levels of insecurity in the job market, made it very difficult for many under 40 to find a first home of their own.

To move from an immediate troubleshooting mode to a proactive housing policy that might work in a more comprehensive fashion took time. The Comuns' policies certainly aimed to be holistic. Their urban planning guidelines identified the unbridled expansion of tourist provision as a major local factor in the process of gentrification that was making rents impossible for residents in several parts of the city and 'expelling' them to more outlying locations, which often meant they needed to devote more time and income to travel to work. By 2016, three-quarters of property sales in the fashionable Eixample district were to foreign buyers; more generally, foreign nationals accounted for 15 per cent of purchases. The city administration had no strategic policy instruments to regulate rent rises, thus it could only apply pressure in relation to rent levels and 'express' eviction procedures brought in by central government, as well as invest in new social housing and urgently address the issue of homelessness.

The most pressing problems related to people facing eviction. A new municipal unit was established to take urgent action as soon as news broke of an impending eviction. This was able to prevent some hundred evictions a month and at least find ways of delaying this outcome or preventing those evicted from ending up on the streets. However, there were still 47 dispossessions a week being reported by May 2019. Lacking legal powers to prevent evictions, the main options open to the administration were checks on whether eviction orders were legally valid, appeals to the social conscience of owners to offer a social housing lease to struggling tenants or alternative accommodation in another empty apartment, and assistance with finding alternative lodgings. The Comuns also established an urban guard unit to combat the practice whereby some owners, seeking to get rid of tenants so that apartments could be upgraded and let to tourists at vastly higher rents, were employing heavies to use intimidation and threats (not to mention rats) to persuade people to leave.

Colau took a personal interest in the growing problem of homelessness, early on spending a night with an NGO monitoring the number of rough sleepers. Her administration spent more on accommodation for those living on the streets, yet homeless numbers continued to rise, not only due to the state of the housing and labour markets but also the pull effect of Barcelona: in May 2018 almost half the newly homeless people were from outside the city and had lived there for less than three months.

To increase social housing provision, the Comuns looked partly to existing potential in the empty apartments used by owners speculatively, tourist apartments that lacked licences to be used for such purposes, the roof space of municipal buildings, such as libraries, schools and markets, and plots between buildings where owners had failed to build. The Colau administration took the view that banks and entrepreneurs involved in the housing market should be given every opportunity to cooperate in finding solutions to problems, believing that they as well as residents stood to benefit. Some bankers, such as the president of CaixaBank, did collaborate in BComú efforts to avoid evictions, but where persuasion failed to convince owners of empty properties to put them on the market or allow them to be used for social housing, the administration used the Law on the Right to Housing to fine banks that had kept properties empty for more than two years; the idea of a tax on empty properties was also considered. Meanwhile individual owners of empty properties (about 70 per cent of such properties) were offered financial incentives to provide social housing for a period of five years and alternatively faced the possibility of prosecution.

One criticism of the Comuns was the amount of time they took in preparing a register of empty properties, although inspection activity greatly increased. In March 2018, with the census still incomplete, an extrapolation from the number of empty apartments detected by municipal inspectors to date suggested that their total was around 13,000, which the Comuns hoped to see added to the social housing stock. Another criticism was that they invested too much hope in efforts to persuade owners of illegal tourist apartments to offer them for social housing in return for having fines commuted: negligible take-up suggested that those benefitting from the illegality were well able to pay fines of between €9,000 and €90,000.

The Colau administration devoted significant resources to the construction of new rented apartment blocks, primarily through the creation of mixed companies to build and manage them. Starting with the identification of land for such projects, this initiative took a long time to deliver: the municipal company to direct this activity was not established until 2018, by which time it was clear that the Comuns would not achieve their target of 8,000 additional apartments (half through new builds, half through purchase) on time. By the end of their term, they had built only 850, bought 700 and received 350 cessions from banks, and another 4,600 were in the pipeline. This was fewer social apartments than the last Socialist-led administration had built, but that was in the context of ongoing PSC municipal control since 1979. Further BComú efforts were made through a new urban planning norm approved in 2018, obliging property developers to devote 30 per cent of new residential and renovation projects to social housing. The Comuns were determined to see it applied across the city, not just in the poorer *barrios*, and across the whole metropolitan area, for which they needed the support of the Generalitat, which faced strong oppositional lobbying from property developers. When Catalan approval of the measure was finally granted in December 2018, this had the potential to add another 300 new social apartments per year.

Funding and the limited policy competence of municipalities in housing were major obstacles here, but in May 2017 the Comuns offset the high cost of new housing developments by securing an EIB credit on advantageous terms, to build some 2,200 apartments. Colau made the point that state expenditure on housing had been cut by 70 per cent under Rajoy and that her administration invested four times as much as the Generalitat on housing, the implication being that if municipal jurisdiction were enhanced (and public financing arrangements adjusted accordingly), so much more could be achieved. Nonetheless, the failure to meet the 8,000 target was something that opposition parties aimed to exploit in the elections.

Criticism of the Comuns' housing record also came from the PAH (Plataforma de Afectados por la Hipoteca, Platform for Mortgage Victims), which described the government's housing measures as 'insufficient' and called for more ambition from the Comuns. This did not end in divorce, however, for they continued to collaborate and in 2018 the administration recruited Colau's successor as PAH spokesman to become an advisor on housing policy and gentrification. It was the PAH and like-minded associations that had taken the initiative of proposing the recent change to the urban planning norms and the Comuns continued to regard such pressure from below as positive and necessary for improving the housing effort. Agitation also came from a new tenants' union, the *Sindicato de Inquilinos*, mobilized by ongoing rent rises, whose creation in 2017 was welcomed by the Comuns. It calculated that rents in the city were exceeding the income of one-third of the population.

Feminization and rights

The Colau administration showed its feminist commitment by introducing gender mainstreaming across all policy areas, ensuring that the views of women were heard in all decision-making processes. It recognized the economic role of carers – most of whom were women – and boosted resources to assist them, partly through the expansion of nursery provision, while in council contracts with companies there was now an insistence on clauses against sexual harassment, codes against homophobia, gender equality plans and measures to close the pay gap. The administration also launched campaigns against *machista* violence, some of them directed at young people. Colau spoke out publicly against sexual harassment, declaring that she had experienced it personally. In March 2018, she took part in one of the biggest demonstrations during the international feminist 'strike', which was particularly well supported in Spain.

The Comuns' radical feminization policies met with resistance, for instance, when the administration tried to persuade public transport entities to make their services sensitive to specific issues concerning the safety of female passengers. Above all, there was resistance within city hall to the Comuns' ambition to close the council pay gap: this could only be pursued with concrete data on pay and it took them four years just to persuade the unions to share it (Pérez interview, 12 April 2019). It proved very difficult, meanwhile, to make municipal politics more accommodative of the circumstances of female councillors with family responsibilities. Colau managed to continue functioning as mayor after becoming a mother for the second time, in April 2017, yet acknowledged that little had been achieved in terms of progress towards family-friendly working hours. Her colleague Laia Ortiz would cite a desire to devote more time to her daughter as a reason for not being available for re-election in 2019.

The Comuns made LGBTI issues a departmental focus linked to feminism for the first time in the city's history. The administration established the first one-stop centre to assist the city's LGBTI community, providing legal and employment advice as well as psychological help. Another area of change was the way the municipal authority dealt with prostitution, by concentrating on the protection of sex workers from exploitation by criminal gangs, rather than criminalizing them. On the International Day of Sex Workers in June 2017, Colau was praised by local organizers for ending fines and the stigma of prostitution, but by the following year she was being criticized by groups in Raval over declining security conditions deemed to be linked to the tolerance of street prostitution.

Migrants were a further specific focus of the rights agenda. The administration acted against leisure centres practising racial discrimination and attempted to help migrants lacking residency papers by introducing a municipal card whereby they could show some evidence of status and possibly persuade judges not to intern them in the city's state-run detention centre. Meanwhile the administration's message to asylum seekers was that they were welcome in Barcelona. Indeed, facilities to receive them were increased, allowing the Catalan capital to play a central role as Spain again became the main European country of arrival for migrants from the south in 2018. Some 11,600 refugees received assistance in Barcelona in 2015–2018.

More generally, BComú developed a more extensive rights agenda than previous administrations had done in Barcelona. Colau's government established a human rights centre and actively promoted it as an opportunity for citizens to seek advice and redress in cases of perceived violations. The city involved itself in the prosecution of policemen accused of violence during the Catalan referendum and showed solidarity with the families of the pro-independence leaders who were jailed while awaiting trial for the challenge to Spanish sovereignty. Several BComú leaders, including deputy mayor Jaume Asens, visited the prisoners and voiced disapproval of their imprisonment.

Mainstreaming the environment

While environmental commitments informed virtually all aspects of BComú policy, the main planks of a campaign to reduce pollution levels were action to reduce the impact of the motor car and energy policy (the latter discussed addressed above under 'Services'). Poor air quality was considered by authorities to be responsible for some 3,500 deaths a year and was thus a major public health issue. Barcelona and Madrid were central to EU concerns about dangerous nitrogen dioxide levels that prompted the European Commission to issue a 'final warning' to Spain in February 2017, threatening action through the European Court of Justice. Barcelona under the Comuns took the lead within Catalonia in responding to this challenge, yet their response was slow to have practical effects and the initial steps taken in 2015–2019 were insufficient to reduce NO_2 emissions.

The premise of BComú was that the car played a disproportionate role in the life of the city, occupying 60 per cent of public space yet accounting for only 26 per cent of journeys. To reduce its role and tackle pollution levels, a raft of measures was introduced by deputy mayor Janet Sanz, responsible for town planning, ecology and mobility: pedestrianization of several areas; the tram project; development of the bicycle network; a ban on high-polluting vehicles from 2020; free public transport passes for owners of high-polluting vehicles prepared to give them up; limits to underground parking permissions in the case of new apartment blocks; higher parking charges on days of especially high pollution; a suspension of licences for new petrol stations in parts of the city; and at metropolitan level a more integrated infrastructure of trains, buses and park-and-ride. These policies were viewed as first steps in what the Comuns hoped would be a long-term strategy, aiming to reduce traffic emissions by 30 per cent over 15 years. This did not have an impact on the number of cars circulating in the city in 2015–2019, partly because of the slow phasing in of the electorally-sensitive issue of car controls. Little was done to reduce the number of cars entering the city, although schemes such as congestion charging in London were being analysed with a view to taking further action in the future.

Like the emissions reduction policy, BComú plans for an overhaul of the rubbish collection system would depend on future administrations. The Comuns envisaged a shift to door-to-door collections, with electronic chips being used to inform the local taxation system and thereby incentivize recycling, while the tendering process would take account of the environmental impact of the vehicles used. Unveiled in 2017, the scheme was initially blocked by the political opposition, demanding further details. Other environmental policies aimed at reducing street noise, through measures such as modifications to pavements and restricting the working hours of cleaning and delivery vehicles; regulating Segways and electric scooters, to protect pedestrians; and liberating the city's beaches by ending some of the concessions to parasol and sunbed businesses, as demanded by local residents.

Resisting the growth of tourism

The expansion of tourism was a matter of high public concern, indeed the main single problem worrying Barcelona's citizens during the second half of 2017, according to the municipal survey known as the Barómetro, before being replaced by Catalonia's relationship to Spain and then the security environment. The administration's desire to curb this growth arose from BComú concerns about sustainability and its ambition to nurture an environment that would serve the needs of residents, first and foremost. The new policy aimed to redirect future hotel construction towards more outlying areas of the city, to alleviate the central concentrations of tourists that caused nuisance to residents and to prevent the local economy becoming 'monocultural' and the city a theme park. The PEUAT (Plan Especial Urbanístico de

Alojamiento, Special Urban Accommodation Plan) sought to modify a situation in which half the beds devoted to tourism were concentrated in just 17 per cent of the city, Ciutat Vella (the district most affected by tourism) had lost one-tenth of its resident population during the tourist boom and rents in the city had risen by 15 per cent in just three years, partly because of the reduced supply of conventional lets. Under BComú, an immediate moratorium was decreed on the granting of licences for all forms of tourist accommodation (hotels, hostels and apartments). It then took a year and a half for the PEUAT to be approved, in January 2017, at which point some 74 hotel projects that already had licences received the go-ahead while another 33 that had been seeking permission were stopped. Hotelier opposition and the influence of the PSC within the coalition brought subsequent modifications, including the removal of a blanket ban on major works in existing hotels in the city centre. Even then, the PEUAT would continue to face legal challenges and in August 2019 these led to a provisional ruling by the Supreme Court of Justice of Catalonia invalidating the plan for lacking an economic assessment (although this had not been required of previous municipal plans).

Previous administrations had seen expansion of the hotel sector as entirely positive and little had been done about the proliferation of tourist apartments, many of which lacked authorization. The Comuns sought to regain municipal powers to issue and withdraw licences for tourist apartments and they used what powers they had to crack down, closing many, fining their owners or initiating procedures to revoke licences for apartments that did not meet municipal requirements. The key to effectiveness was detection activity. This had begun at the end of the Trias administration and was greatly stepped up by the Comuns, who followed up denunciations made by residents' associations in the *barrios* where these apartments were located. BComú's *bête noire* was Airbnb, which, along with other digital platforms, had been advertising apartments in the tourist market without checking whether they had licences to function for this purpose. Both Airbnb and HomeAway were fined by the Colau administration for advertising unauthorized apartments and eventually agreed to stop doing so in cases whose illegality had been exposed by the city authorities. By August 2017, the council had taken legal action against more than 6,000 properties used as tourist apartments while lacking a licence; by March 2019 it had closed over 3,000 illegal tourist apartments and claimed to have cut the supply by 95 per cent – a figure disputed by neighbourhood associations in La Barceloneta.

Another major concern of the Comuns was the growing impact of cruise ships. Here they had less power to act autonomously, so placed their emphasis on problematizing the phenomenon and lobbying for concerted action, while exploring the possibility of an additional tax for cruise liners on top of the tourist tax. Barcelona's sea passenger numbers reached almost 4 million in 2016, of which 2.7 million were cruise passengers and the rest mostly ferry passengers. Port authority figures showed cruise passengers to be bigger spenders than other tourists. While their presence was welcomed by the city's travel agents, luxury retailers, restauranteurs and taxi firms, it was bemoaned by many residents owing to the problems caused by crowds in particular areas. The Colau administration reached an agreement with the Port of Barcelona to concentrate cruiser ship terminals on a quay away from the city, but this was opposed by the normally sympathetic Federation of Barcelona Residents Associations (FAVB) which feared that the number of cruisers would increase.

Overall, the Comuns' measures had the greatest impact on the regulation of tourist apartments. In contrast, the volume of hotel accommodation continued to grow, owing to licences that had been granted before the PEUAT took effect, but the latter did bring a fall in the number of requests to build new hotels, prompting complaints from hotel chains that the sector would lose global competitiveness. Visitor numbers also continued to grow under the Comuns, reaching over 30 million a year, notwithstanding the events of 2017 (the terrorist attack in August and the political instability and confrontations associated with the independence referendum), from which the luxury hotels suffered most in lost bookings. Instability was also a factor in the failure of the Catalan bid to have the European Medicines Agency relocated to Barcelona and the loss of the Barcelona World Race, a round-the-world yacht race that previously had brought €23 million to the city.

Residents groups in some *barrios* continued to stage protests over the negative impact of tourism and in 2017 the militant pro-independence youth organization Arran staged violent attacks on some hotels: a campaign that some business voices attributed to a hostility towards tourism that they claimed had been fostered by the Comuns, despite BComú's condemnation of the violence. The ability of any municipal government in Barcelona to regulate tourism was limited, of course, yet the fact that a major effort was being made to manage it prompted criticism both from those wounded by regulation and those wanting more drastic action. Those opposing BComú's tourism policy from the business sector were its natural political opponents in any case. More crucial for the Comuns, as election time drew near, was whether criticisms of their policy performance regarding tourism would undermine their credibility within their own electoral space.

Global outreach

The Comuns came into office as critics of a global capitalism whose benefits were seen to be excessively confined to economic elites. They aimed to change the business-driven orientation of Barcelona's participation in the international economic system by gradually transforming the city in accordance with their social and environmental values, while at the same time promoting these values externally by means of the international outreach of the city. As with earlier social democratic experiments, gradualism involved considerable initial accommodations with the existing order, in order to avoid the financial disruption that more radical policies would have implied. Colau and her colleagues had been outspoken opponents of the World Mobile Congress (WMC), yet in office immediately extended the city's contract to host it for another eight years. Not only did the event generate income for the city (€465 million in 2017): the 108,000 participants belonging to 200 nationalities also created 13,000 temporary jobs each year. BComú's attitude was not exactly 'business as usual', however. As mentioned earlier, at its meeting in 2018, Colau together with the president of the Catalan Parliament, Roger Torrent, risked adding to the organizers' concerns about Catalonia's recent political instability by boycotting the official reception for the Spanish King.

The Comuns did demonstrate a distinctive approach to the kind of global city that Barcelona should become. In contrast to the Trias administration, they were deeply critical of the neo-liberal concept of smart cities, based on the growing importance of information and communication technologies, regarding this as being market-driven by competitiveness, rather than promoting international cooperation, and as seeking to make cities serve the needs of international capital rather than their people. In April 2016, plans for Barcelona to host a UN Habitat conference on smart cities were vetoed by the Colau administration, which managed to refocus the event onto issues of public space and the right of citizens to their city. The theme was that in thriving cities such as Barcelona, public space was coming increasingly under pressure and municipal action was imperative to counteract the trend. Colau's speech held that cities should be viewed as more than agglomerations of homes and services and that public space should be used to promote social cohesion, equal opportunities and democracy. Barcelona went on to host the Smart City World Congress in November 2018, its focus being on improvements in living conditions.

Nonetheless, a degree of continuity with the existing global orientations of the city was seen in the Comuns' ambition for Barcelona to remain a leader in the world of ICT. In February 2018, building on the WMC foundation, Colau spoke of the city's objective to become a global hub for the revolutionary 5G technology that would be introduced in the near future. In the same year, Barcelona was chosen by Facebook as the location for a new centre to combat fake news. Meanwhile, new directions for the city, as a place enhancing the lives of its residents, were pursued through various programmes and events. A lot of activity was organized around the theme of 'fearless cities', 'standing up to defend human rights, democracy and the common good'. BComú hosted an initial meeting of the global municipalist movement in June 2017 and similar conferences ensued in New York City, Warsaw, Brussels and Valparaíso. A new website described the goal of the participants as being that of 'radicalizing democracy, feminizing politics and standing up to the far right', and described them as seeking to build 'global networks of solidarity and hope from the bottom up' (www.fearlesscities.com). A 'fearless cities' symposium organized by the Democratic Party in New York in July 2018 saw further consolidation of these links, not least with Congressional candidate Alexandria Ocasio-Cortez, like Colau, another young female politician who had come from the social movements, and who was later elected in the mid-term elections in November. This forum became an outspoken critic of Donald Trump, seen as a dangerous threat to rights and freedoms. The 'fearless cities' theme was multidimensional in its range and broad enough to accommodate many of the global objectives of the Comuns. However, its name, which many took to imply an effort to make cities a safer place in which to live, became a hostage to fortune as public security concerns became a difficult electoral issue for BComú towards the end of their term in office.

Following in the footsteps of Pasqual Maragall, Colau undertook a very active international role personally to promote the policies of her administration and develop global collaborations. An official visit to New York in May 2016 was based on common concerns about inequality, property speculation and the impact of tourism, and led to a cooperation agreement. Several early visits formed part of the build-up to the Habitat III summit, the UN Conference on Housing and Sustainable Development that took place in Quito later that year, with Colau speaking in the opening session. Cooperation agreements were signed too with Paris mayor Anne Hidalgo, with whom Colau shared a commitment to the feminization of political life. Barcelona's representative also featured prominently in a summit of European mayors held at the Vatican in December 2016 to discuss the refugee crisis; it called for cities to be granted greater powers over the reception of refugees, particularly those coming from Syria. The Comuns branded Barcelona a 'city of refuge' and here again risked falling short when it came to delivery, given the very limited municipal powers in this domain. In July 2016, Colau faced noisy hecklers demanding the closure of the state-run migrant detention centre in Barcelona, when she went to inaugurate a public display monitoring the number of migrant deaths at sea in the Mediterranean, and the city was able to welcome very few refugees in the early part of her administration. However, once state policy towards migrants was modified by Pedro Sánchez in 2018, Barcelona under the Comuns proceeded to take the lead among Spanish municipalities in accommodating many of the new wave of asylum seekers who had been arriving in Andalucía by sea.

Rather than seeking to build a new left-wing International, BComú's international activity was ends-based. It involved particularly close collaboration with comparable movements in places such as Naples, Grenoble, Valparaíso, Jackson (Mississippi), Amsterdam and Montreal, many of which approached the Comuns initially to draw lessons from their electoral triumph; but there was also cooperation with more politically dissimilar municipal authorities based on tackling specific challenges, such as housing. Equally, pragmatism often led the Comuns to seek the involvement of the most strategically important cities, such as New York, London and Paris, in major international initiatives (Shea Baird interview, 21 May 2018). Meanwhile, the Comuns intervened influentially in the main global association of city, local and regional governments, United Cities and Local Government (UCLG), of which Colau became a vice-president in 2016. UCLG, in which more than 1,000 cities are represented, and Metropolis, the main network of metropolitan areas, share global headquarters in Barcelona, and the city has participated actively too in Eurocities, the principal European network. It was partly through such associations and through the 'Cities without Fear' programme that Barcelona returned to international prominence under the Comuns, while Colau herself became an internationally recognized political figure. In 2016, Politico judged her to be the most influential Spaniard in Europe and ranked her fifth in a list of 28 people, headed by Sadiq Khan, deemed likely to shape the continent in 2017 (www.politico.eu, 12 August 2016).

Security challenges

Public security had not been prioritized in BComú's electoral programme, even though the growth of tourism had brought increases in illegality – unlicensed street sellers, petty theft, street prostitution and the drugs trade – especially in districts such as Ciutat Vella. Security issues affected the public spaces that the Comuns wanted to reclaim, restore and improve for the citizens, yet this subject received few references in the electoral programme, such as a vague commitment to improve community policing. BComú held that the role of policing should not be limited to maintaining public order and taking measures to avoid crime: it should help safeguard 'plural security' by prioritizing the weak and vulnerable as part of a project addressing basic living conditions and recognizing people's dignity. The only specific commitments were to redeploy the anti-riot unit of the local police (Guardia Urbana) and to create an observatory on human rights that would incorporate the tasks of a police complaints commission (Barcelona en Comú, 2015: 47–48). The tensions between social movements and the Guardia over recent years – when the latter along with the Catalan Mossos d'Esquadra had been involved in action against squatters – were translated into cool, mutual suspicion between the police and the new administration.

The Comuns proceeded to reform the Guardia by decentralizing it, neutralizing its anti-riot capacity and eventually abolishing the anti-riot unit. This meant that, if mediation failed, any police action to end occupations came to depend on the Mossos. In May 2016, the local police force complained about political interference, following an attempt to seek the release from custody of a street vendor accused of assaulting a policeman. Relations between police forces and the political authorities in Catalonia were being strained also in the context of the independence movement's use of mass mobilization to build support. Eventually the police began to mobilize themselves to express their own grievances, starting with a demonstration in January 2017 which had support from both the local and Catalan forces.

The issue of the *top manta* – street vendors from Sub-Saharan Africa congregating to set up often quite large makeshift markets to sell fake merchandise without authorization in busy public places – shows the evolution of the administration's policing policy. The Comuns saw these *manteros* as a vulnerable group of migrants, exploited by the mafias that supplied them and simply trying to make a living through mutual support (Serra Carné, 2016: 178). BComú sought to end the use of punitive measures and find legal economic activities that would remove *mantero* concentrations from tourist hotspots, where there could be risks to public safety, especially when police operations led to street chases. Initially Colau's administration reduced police foot patrols against the *top manta* and tried to redirect vendors towards a special job training programme. By mid-2018, some 130 youths had abandoned street selling, mostly to work in cooperatives created by the council, but the phenomenon persisted, partly because many migrants continued to lack residency permits, tourist numbers continued to increase and the city was only one of several Catalan holiday destinations in which the *top manta* operated. This was an issue that brought criticism of the administration from diverse quarters: from social movements protesting over the abuse of public space (notably the residents' association of La Barceloneta), shop owners and the political opposition, not least the CUP. Retailers complained about the 'unfair competition' they faced from this activity and the fact that Colau herself only met their representatives some three years into her administration.

The Comuns eventually managed to reduce the number of street vendors, but this was partly by restoring police patrols in the areas affected (often in combination with other police units), thereby tacitly accepting the shortcomings of the social/tolerant approach to the issue. A further programme subsidized by the council aimed to channel *manteros* into shop employment from June 2018. Tolerance meanwhile was seen also in the Comuns' response to protest camps set up in central plazas in support of the homeless or to apply pressure in support of the independence challenge, yet eventually the Guardia would be used, or intervention by the Mossos sought, when such camps began to affect other activities.

From 2017, the Colau administration called for a greater police presence in parts of the city and more effective collaboration from the Generalitat. It was spending a lot more on police overtime itself and looked to the Catalan government to increase its contribution to policing the city. Not only had some concentrations of *manteros* reappeared as soon as the Mossos had been withdrawn following a clampdown the previous year: there were other security challenges too that were rising up the evolving policy agenda. The most dramatic challenge came from terrorism, which hit the city and the Catalan coastal town of Cambrils in August through the agency of Jihadi militants. Barcelona proved highly vulnerable, especially to the van attack on La Rambla, where 13 pedestrians were killed and 130 injured. There were certainly security lessons to be learnt, although not by the administration alone, for decisions on terrorism prevention were the responsibility of a committee on which all the police agencies were involved. The outcome was one of unity against terrorism rather than attempts to capitalize politically on the failings.

Meanwhile, during 2018, city crime figures worsened, notably robberies and thefts in the historic centre of the city, Ciutat Vella, where there were local protests, although not supported by the more senior residents' associations or the FAVB. In October, Colau's pressure for more Catalan action finally led to massive raids by 700 Mossos in the *barrio* of Raval, aimed against *narcopisos*; and months later there were joint police operations to remove concentrations of *manteros* from metro stations. Colau's view was that the only effective way to tackle the latter challenge was for central government to entitle migrants lacking residency permits to pursue legitimate employment opportunities.

During the final year of Colau's administration, there was deep disunity among the municipal parties over security challenges, apart from an eventual agreement between BComú and the PDeCAT (Partit Demòcrata Europeu Català, Catalan European Democratic Party) on measures against *narcopisos*. Drugs-related security challenges seemed to be growing, or at least were presented as such, as most of the opposition parties saw the security domain as providing their main chance of success in the next municipal election. Having defeated the *multiconsulta* in April 2018, all except the CUP demanded a debate on the 'degradation' of Ciutat Vella, citing the proliferation of *narcopisos* in Raval, the existence of protest camps in Plaça de Catalunya, civil insecurity, attacks on tourist infrastructure and the *top manta*. This resulted in a formal reproof for the mayor and attempts to force her to give up personal responsibility for security. The pressure was aimed at securitizing all discussion of the problems and attributing rising crime levels to policy failings on the part of the administration, although the problems went well beyond the municipal domain and the competences of the municipal authority and its police force. Nonetheless, by putting more emphasis on the need for the Generalitat to increase the number of Mossos in the city, Colau appeared to be tacitly acknowledging that the Comuns had got the policy mix wrong insofar as security was concerned. By January 2019, with the municipal barometer showing insecurity to have become the main cause of public concern in Barcelona, it was a key area of vulnerability for BComú as it prepared for the forthcoming elections. Better news about city burglary figures came only after the election, in June.

6   Comuns in Catalonia
Failing to take off?

It was never going to be easy for the Comuns to grow outwards from Barcelona and establish a presence across Catalonia, for various reasons. Since the immediate focus was on winning seats in the Catalan Parliament and changing the political orientation of the Generalitat, one obstacle was simply the frequency of regional elections. The Catalan election of December 2017 was the fourth to be held (three of them early) in seven years; thus the time between creating a new party and preparing for an election was likely to be extremely short. The task was that much greater for those who aspired to build a citizen-based political option rather than an elite party. It would be especially difficult to introduce a grassroots organization and develop confluence politics in a much larger, politically diverse territory such as Catalonia and – for a party of the left – in a period when the independence movement was reaching a crescendo in terms of popular support. Yet intervention at the Catalan level was something that BComú saw as an urgent priority, given the limits to municipal policy competences and its antipathy towards what it saw as the centre-right orientations of the successive Puigdemont and Torra governments.

Catalunya en Comú (CatComú) was announced on 19 December 2016, founded in an Assembly on 8 April 2017 and contested its first elections as part of a CatComú-Podem list the following December. The aim was to go beyond the traditional pattern of left-wing alliances which had its most recent expression in the ICV-EUiA-Podem combination CSQP (Catalunya Sí que es Pot, Catalonia Yes We Can) that had entered the 2015 election. CatComú's ambition to develop as a confluence implied qualitative progress in terms of unification, yet thus far it has fallen short when compared with BComú, and indeed by 2019 these were still very different organizations, with CatComú more reliant on top-down efforts and less well embedded in society. In 2017, it won fewer seats than ICV-EUiA or CSQP in recent elections to the Catalan Parliament, although it did find itself holding the balance of power therein. In the parliament eventually constituted in 2018, CatComú-Podem was the only group straddling the Catalan divide over independence. Its hybridity in this regard has not proved as damaging to internal cohesion as it did to CSQP, whose election list had been based entirely on party quotas; however, it still proved problematic, both in that election and following the electoral disappointment. At the Catalan level, there is still an open question as to whether confluence approaches can work any better than alliance strategies when it comes to the navigation of internal diversity regarding the national question.

Failure of the old alliance approach

Collaboration between left parties involved new challenges by 2017, both because of the salience of the Catalan independence issue, over which the left was divided, and the recent participation of social movement activists in political life, bringing different perspectives. BComú refrained from joining CSQP because its own entry into municipal life was so recent and there was no time to develop a process of confluence at the Catalan level following the calling of an early election by Artur Mas in September 2015 (Russo Spena and Forti, 2016: 138–139). Besides, the election had been called in order to seek a mandate for an independence push. An improvised response was never going to be convincing to an electorate that, in any case, had demonstrated less propensity to vote along right-left lines in elections to the Catalan Parliament. Securing just 11 seats in this election, two fewer than ICV-EUiA in 2012, was already a recipe for internal CSQP friction.

BComú's misgivings about CSQP were borne out by the increasingly visible tensions within the new parliamentary group within which there were two independents (including group president Lluís Rabell), four deputies each from ICV (Iniciativa per Catalunya Verds, Initiative for Catalonia Greens) and Podem and one from EUiA (Esquerra Unida i Alternativa, United Left and Alternative). From the start, there was much rivalry over group representation. Lacking a strong leader, CSQP cohesion suffered from lingering Podem doubts about ICV as a partner and what it saw as the dominant role of that party in practice through Joan Coscubiela being spokesperson. Although Albano Dante Fachin of Podem was allocated the post of co-spokesperson, the media tended to contact Coscubiela for statements. The arrangement proved problematic since Fachin, especially following his victory in primaries for Podem secretary-general in October 2015, resisted subordination and was keen to impress his own party's brandmark on any collaborative efforts in Catalonia. Exacerbated by the existence of factionalism within Podem, there were 'intolerable constant tensions' and power struggles, at the expense of political discussion, within the CSQP group (Albiach interview, 25 May 2018).

As the independence process unfolded, CSQP proved unable to agree on a response to the ultimately unilateralist road map advanced by the independence parties, once efforts to secure central government consent for a referendum had failed. The whole group believed that a referendum lacking international recognition and inclusiveness could be neither legally nor politically effective, yet its demand for prior recognition of the referendum by the Venice Commission of the Council of Europe was asking for the impossible, given that this body was to be expected to defend the Spanish Constitution and government. By October 2016, CSQP had decided that a referendum negotiated with the Rajoy government was impossible, but it still had difficult tactical decisions to take over how to proceed as the plans to hold it went ahead unilaterally. The only internal compromise the group could reach was a politically weak, ultimately unsustainable one: to abstain in parliamentary votes in order to avoid exposing its own disunity.

The outstanding contours of internal disputes showed Coscubiela and other ICV deputies wanting to vote against moves by the pro-independence majority in Parliament towards holding a referendum, whereas Podem's deputies were inclined to facilitate such an event while describing it as just a 'mobilization' of Catalan public opinion whose results would not have legal force. Often acting as an umpire between the two and counselling abstention in parliamentary votes on this issue, communist leader Joan Josep Nuet (EUiA) also wielded influence as the group's representative on the parliamentary management committee, where his vote facilitated the tabling of the independence plans for debate. CSQP attempted to steer a mid-course between independence parties and unionists, but proved unable to maintain it unitedly as public opinion over a unilateral referendum became sharply polarized.

The crunch came on 7 September 2017 when Coscubiela spoke out as a strict defender of legality and the rights of the parliamentary minority, opposed to the 'express' procedural moves used by the independence parties to gain the Catalan Parliament's approval of the referendum and transition laws that finally set Catalonia on the path to a referendum on 1 October. He received an unprecedented ovation from PSC, PP and Cs deputies, but his own group was now in tatters. While a majority, including Jéssica Albiach of Podem, joined him in voting against a proposal to change the parliamentary agenda in order to vote on the two laws, seeing this as an undemocratic manoeuvre by the independence parties, Fachin and two other Podem deputies abstained, partly to avoid alignment with the unionist parties but also to protest about the insistence by Coscubiela on monopolizing the group's time allocation during a crucial parliamentary session (Serra Carné and González, 2017: 100). With Podem prevented from expressing its views, Fachin proceeded to call publicly for Coscubiela's replacement. Later, the latter described the turbulent parliamentary sessions of 6–7 September as a 'spectacular process of political degradation and national regression' and stated that a majority of the group had wanted to oppose the referendum law itself, but had abstained in an attempt to maintain group discipline (*El Periódico*, 6 September 2018).

CSQP finally disintegrated during the events that followed the referendum. On 26 October, when the Catalan Parliament held a secret ballot on a resolution to declare independence, the group attempted to vote against it. After its approval by 70–10 votes with 2 abstentions (some opposition deputies being absent), it was not entirely clear how some individual group members had behaved since only seven revealed how they had voted while Fachin, Joan Giner and Àngels Martínez Castells of Podem did not, nor did Nuet. Fachin explained that this minority had not wanted to help implicate the pro-independence deputies who had voted yes, but he could not mitigate the impression of political incoherence that had been given.

In Common We Can

CSQP had been an improvised, incomplete coalition of forces to the left of the Socialists, broad enough, however, to embrace crippling differences in the context of a Catalan Parliament centrally concerned with the independence issue. The entry of the Comuns into Spanish state-wide politics later in 2015 brought a much more effective electoral alliance in the form of En Comú Podem (ECP, In Common We Can). This alliance presented itself as belonging to the broad Catalan tradition of secular republicanism, its ideal being a Catalan republic that would federate with a Spanish republic (Russo Spena and Forti, 2016: 140–141; Domènech, 2016) and strive to imprint a progressive orientation on both. It was led by a unitary figure in the form of historian Xavier Domènech and was backed unreservedly by Ada Colau and Pablo Iglesias, thus enabling ECP to be associated with both the popularity of the Colau administration in Barcelona and the rise of Podemos as a new radical force in Spanish politics. ECP successes in the general elections of December 2015 and June 2016 should be seen too in the context of a traditional Catalan propensity to favour the left in Spanish elections.

ECP did especially well in 2015, winning almost 928,000 votes (24.7 per cent), compared with the 366,000 that had been won by CSQP in September. This was its first victory across Catalonia, rewarded with 12 of the 47 Catalan seats in the Congress of Deputies, 9 of them representing Barcelona province (total 31) and 1 each for Tarragona, Girona and Lleida. It also won four seats in the Senate. ICV-EUiA had won only three seats in the Spanish election of 2011. The results of this broader alliance were extremely encouraging. ECP's demand for a negotiated referendum within a year attracted voters – including some who had backed independence parties in September – who had doubts about the unilateralist road map and considered a negotiated referendum to be still possible. Podemos and its allies now had 69 seats in Congress (27 of them won through regionally-based lists, such as ECP) and were pressing hard for the formation of a left-wing coalition committed to constitutional reform. As ERC leader Oriol Junqueras pointed out, however, Spanish parties opposed to the negotiation of a referendum – including the PSOE (Partido Socialista Obrero Español, Spanish Socialist Workers' Party) – still had 70 per cent of the seats in parliament, a fact brought home to ECP when it was prevented from forming a separate parliamentary group in Madrid, on the grounds that the regional lists had not competed against Podemos in the election.

Disagreements over Catalonia featured prominently in the failed efforts of PSOE leader Pedro Sánchez to form a coalition in 2015–2016, one of several obstacles being that ECP demanded a commitment to a referendum in return for assisting in his investiture bid. This was not forthcoming, although PSC leader Miquel Iceta did suggest that if the Spanish parliamentary arithmetic prevented constitutional reform, another way forward might be a referendum law based on the way that Canada had addressed the Quebec issue. During the election campaign, Colau herself had spoken of the possibility of a referendum with several questions, thus showing flexibility on her part, yet the bottom line for the Comuns was one that the PSOE would not accept: that the question of independence was an issue that Catalan voters should be allowed to decide upon.

When Spanish voters were called to the polls again on 26 June 2016, following the failure of coalition efforts, ECP again triumphed in Catalonia. A recent Metroscopia poll (*El País*, 31 May 2016) had underlined its widespread popularity in the province of Barcelona, where it was attracting greater support than its rivals among every age group except the over-65s (where PSC-PSOE preferences prevailed). Particularly high support among 18–34-year-olds augured well for the future of the Comuns. ECP's result, however, proved disappointing, indicating consolidation rather than growth. On a lower turnout, its vote fell from 928,000 to 848,000 while its share remained constant at 24 per cent. The disappointment was threefold: (1) the left's defeat in the election; (2) the alternative left's failure to overtake the PSOE despite Podemos, the regional lists and IU having formed a new electoral alliance, Unidos Podemos (UP) (Gillespie, 2017b); and (3) the evidence that ECP's referendum position was not resonating more strongly now among Catalan voters. Looking to expand beyond Barcelona, ECP had put greater efforts into contesting Girona and Lleida, but these provinces continued to support independence parties and electoral gains made by ERC showed that the unilateral road map was still supported by many Catalans. Although ECP's vote increased outside of Barcelona, it won no additional seats there and remained on 12 seats. The election suggested that the task of extending the influence of the Comuns from their Barcelona heartland to other parts of Catalonia would require a long, difficult struggle accompanied by organizational growth.

Creating Catalonia en Comú

The main difference between CatComú and these electoral alliances was the idea of creating a common party that would seek to establish an organized citizen base in society, rather than simply proceeding through a series of elite negotiations between party leaders. The process began, certainly, in traditional fashion with talks between the four main political components of BComú and with some notion of maintaining a balance between them. It was these organizations that would collectively steer the foundation process and produce the original draft of a political position document for discussion and amendment, but thereafter the process would be extended both to their own activists and to members of the public wishing to take part in the discussion, before eventually – after much amendment of the document – it would be adopted and a leadership selected at an open founding assembly. The decision to proceed with the initiative was announced by Colau in January 2016, the recent general election victory of ECP serving as a catalyst while her own involvement in the project helped persuade activists that they could now form an effective Catalan party, with more electoral appeal than the earlier efforts made by offshoots from the traditional communist movement.

At this time, a parallel process of leadership succession and party renewal imbued ICV with fresh enthusiasm for a Catalan confluence, while it also had financial difficulties that made its separate party development problematic. It envisaged the new confluence space functioning as a kind of 'political cooperative' in which existing party activists and newcomers would collaborate and nobody would be more important than anyone else. EUiA had meanwhile decided that this proposed party was the 'new political subject' they had been speaking about for years (Salado interview, 9 April 2019). As for Podem, the party with the strongest organizational involvement at the Spanish level, it was divided and lacking leadership following the resignation of secretary-general Gemma Ubasart the previous autumn; initially, it was thus less assertive of a distinctive position, yet eventually would become the major obstacle to the foundation process. All four components, including BComú, were now ready to engage in some form of confluence politics at the Catalan level, but there remained a debate – for some to do with timescale – about whether the new party should come to supersede the constituent parties.

After an initial phase of internal, separate party-based debates, BComú took steps to bring the discussion together and agree on a road map for the confluence process. In July it received internal endorsement for a working paper setting out the programmatic premises for a pro-sovereignty Catalan party of the left, based on four areas: (1) the model for a new Catalonia; (2) human and social rights; (3) a defence of common goods; and (4) sovereignty and Spanish 'plurinationality'. It decided on its own representatives to take forward the proposal by creating a steering group with the other parties to work on an initial manifesto, which subsequently would give rise to a larger promoting body and broader discussion. Through the presence of existing parties within such bodies, BComú's partners were reassured that they would retain some control over the process, particularly in the early phases when the basic parameters of the new project were decided. The partners welcomed the fact that BComú had taken the steering wheel to set the vehicle in motion, but each would continue to have its own debates about the direction to be followed and would have its own proposals, plus some red lines. A substantial degree of unity was seen in October 2016 when all four parties rebuffed the interest showed by the Catalan Socialists in an electoral alliance with the nascent party, for neither Iceta's short-lived advocacy of the Canadian model of addressing the national question nor his party's ideas for a federal Spanish constitutional reform satisfied their own demands for a Catalan right to decide.

The constituent process moved up a gear in December when the steering group agreed on a provisional name, 'A Country in Common', and on a document providing an outline of the new party's political ideas, among them, the desire to achieve Catalan sovereignty in economic, environmental and social as well as political institutional terms, and a call for subsidiarity within the sovereignty debate: 'municipalism is in our DNA' (Un País en Comú, 2017: 53–55). This was the point at which the discussion was opened to Catalan society to join the debate, through the establishment of both a website and a promoting body of over 100 people, the majority drawn from outside the political party stratosphere. Some 375 activists and experts were consulted while drafting the political document, over 2,000 contributions were made to its elaboration, and some 3,500 were involved in the ensuing debate, either in person or online (ibid.: 3).

Negotiations between the parties became more difficult from early 2017, largely because of developments within Podemos. Divided through alignment with the different positions defended by secretary-general Pablo Iglesias, the more moderate political secretary Íñigo Errejón and the 'anti-capitalist' tendency led by MEP Miguel Urbán, there were additional tensions arising from Podem's efforts to assert a degree of political sovereignty within Podemos, the existence in Catalonia of an anti-capitalist majority critical of the Podemos leadership and the controversial behaviour of Podem secretary-general Fachin, who backed Iglesias at the second congress of Podemos (Vistalegre II) despite being a member of the anti-capitalist tendency. When the *pablista* position (i.e., that of Pablo Iglesias) triumphed there in February, in votes in which some 15,000 Podem supporters took part, Fachin felt authorized to press for a greater say in the Catalan confluence negotiations, claiming that the popularity of Podemos among the less Catalanist part of the electorate in metropolitan Barcelona would be crucial in elections (Subirats interview, 7 April 2017). Eventually offered more than a quarter of the seats on the list for the executive (more than any other party), Fachin pressed for more, aiming to have veto power, but this was rejected (Nuet interview, 6 April 2017). His executive wanted Podem's own brand to become the matrix of the new party, reflected in its name, whereas others wanted the new entity to be a discrete, common construct (Lo Cascio interview, 22 May 2018; Albiach interview, 25 May 2018).

This remained the fundamental sticking point, even if more specific differences were raised. Fachin wanted to see an unequivocal statement on the right to decide, rather than one designed to accommodate the federalist views of majorities within the post-communist parties (Salado interview, 11 November 2016; Cid interview, 9 November 2016). However, several of the issues he raised involved distortions of his interlocutors' positions, perhaps to rally support for his leadership within Podem; and his call on the Comuns for Podem to be allowed to participate in common decisions via its own online register of supporters fuelled suspicions that for him this was a power struggle, to ensure that the new party would bear the hallmarks of Podemos. Podem claimed to have 52,000 *inscritos*, of whom some 28,000 were 'active', in the limited sense of having taken part in a recent online internal consultation or assembly; Fachin contrasted this with a figure of 2,000 members participating in the primaries held by other confluence parties, among which the post-communist parties continued to have more demanding notions of membership. While Podemos and BComú made a distinction between *activistas* and *inscritos*, the other two parties operated with categories based on the traditional distinction on the left between members and sympathizers, of which ICV had 4,358 and 1,520 respectively and EUiA 3,542 and 2,509 (*El País*, 1 March 2017). When Fachin's executive eventually consulted its *inscritos* over whether to take part in the founding assembly of the new confluence, only 3,901 votes were cast, of which 2,424 (60.5 per cent) supported Podem's executive in opposing it. Over time, its online participation levels varied widely depending on the issue concerned: over 17,000 would vote in a consultation on whether to ally with CatComú in the Catalan election of December 2017. Measured against neo-Leninist standards, Podem probably had closer to 1,000 activists (off-the-record interview with Podem member, May 2018).

After Podem's consultation on participation in the Assembly, further concessions were made to its demands in efforts to persuade it to reconsider. Ultimately, however, Fachin decided to boycott the event, declaring that his conditions had not been met. This did not prevent Podem activists from participating as individuals, but it did mean that the unitary enterprise would be incomplete and thus the new party would need to hold one-on-one negotiations with Podem to form an electoral alliance or would fail to maximize its electoral potential. The Podem saga had monopolized media coverage of the party construction process, ignoring debates on policy issues, feminism, common goods, the role of the state and Europe – on which support for the EU prevailed, albeit with criticisms (Lo Cascio interview, 22 May 2018).

Fachin was not alone in criticizing the construction process. A minority within EUiA complained of a lack of democratic transparency, with some justification. Moreover, only to a limited degree were the Comuns following new politics principles through developing the confluence on the basis of individual incorporation and without strict quotas for the representation of constituent parties on steering and coordination bodies: some degree of party political balance was impli-cit – enough for critics to suspect that informal quotas had been agreed. When Domènech as coordinator presented his own lists of candidates for the 32-member executive and 120-member coordinating body in March 2017, he responded to the balance of forces challenge by proposing that half the places be allocated to non-party indepen-dents, in order to attract and appeal to people with different profes-sional skills and backgrounds across a wider swathe of society. His executive list included five people from ICV, four each from BComú and EUiA, seven from dissident sectors of Podem, as well as several individuals who had worked closely with him or Colau. There were three rival lists, among them an incomplete one presented by Podem members headed by Jéssica Albiach and Marc Bartolomeu, who were critical of Fachin's behaviour in the negotiations.

The election results for the leadership bodies suggest that, at the outset, the number of people responding to appeals to join was no greater than the aggregated numbers involved in the constituent par-ties. This does not mean that it attracted exactly the same people: rather, numerically, the newcomers were cancelled out by a proportion of existing activists who chose not to take part. In all, 9,279 people registered, of whom 6,805 proceeded to have their ID verified so that they could participate in voting, and 5,540 voted in the leadership elections, which began online before the Assembly took place. Some 2,000 people attended the event itself, in the Vall d'Hebron Pavilion, among them Podemos number two Pablo Echenique, who had attempted a last-minute mediation with Podem. The numbers were respectable if one bears in mind three factors: (1) the decline in social mobilization since the creation of Procès Constituent and Guanyem Barcelona in 2013–2014; (2) the greater salience now of the indepen-dence question in Catalan politics; and (3) the impact of party fac-tionalism, especially within Podemos. What was less satisfactory for the Comuns was the breakdown of the votes within the winning list for the executive, a system of open lists having been adopted in response to demands from Podem. This revealed particularly high voting for ICV members, leading Nuet to estimate that up to 800 participants may have voted along party lines rather than in accordance with the Comuns' mantra that representatives should be chosen on the basis of individual contribution (Serra Carné and González, 2017: 141–147).

The political resolution approved at the Assembly outlined a vision of Catalonia becoming a social and democratic republic, freely sharing sovereignty with a plurinational Spain. Although some participants advocated a confederal Spain, the formula chosen implied a federal state with some confederal features, not least in its relationship with Catalonia. An amendment specifying that Catalonia had to become a state in order to attain sovereignty was defeated by 1,125 to 148 (plus 67 blank) votes, while a federalist amendment was rejected by 960 to 300 (and 98 blank) votes. Online voting on the sensitive issue of the name of the new party was scheduled for the days following the Assembly: it came down to a choice between the existing En Comú Podem used in general elections and Catalunya en Comú, the latter being chosen by 53.7 per cent, thus resolving the issue of whether association with Podem should be highlighted. The name chosen referred to Catalonia as the political focus, evoked the protagonism of BComú and hinted at the party's commitment to new politics.

In July, when CatComú's coordinating body adopted a position in support of the referendum announced by Puigdemont for 1 October, it seemed that internal compromise on this issue, and with Podem, was possible. Some 85 of its members voted for the resolution, describing the referendum as a legitimate affirmation of the right to decide, but considering it (as Podem did) only a 'legitimate mobilization' – not the referendum that Catalonia needed. A minority (29) backed an alternative resolution deeming the planned referendum to be an 'effective' one and committing the party to alignment with the pro-independence parties. However, when several CatComú leaders (including Domènech, Nuet and Elisenda Alamany) proceeded to state individually that they intended to vote in the referendum, the federalist current within the party – mostly formed by ICV members – felt that this was inconsistent with what had been decided. They began to act autonomously. July also saw the publication of a manifesto by 200 activists (growing subsequently to 300) giving reasons why they would boycott the referendum. A consultation of CatComú *inscritos* in September then endorsed participation, the prevailing argument being that the event had been legitimized effectively by the repressive response of the PP: 3,457 (59.4 per cent, or 44 per cent of the total register) voted yes to taking part.

Momentarily, there still seemed to be a coherent majority within CatComú, based on the supporters of pro-sovereignty and federalist formulas. Once Puigdemont had clarified his plans for the referendum and the Colau administration in Barcelona had agreed to facilitate voting, however, the majority began to erode. CatComú was becoming involved with the event but remained opposed to the independence objective and unilateralism. This was a position that disappointed both the pro-independence and the unionist camps in Catalonia, while exacerbating tensions within the Comuns. Confluence principles involved the gradual building and maintenance of consensus through discussion and common activity over time, yet events were now moving very fast and, in the context of a polarized battle, formulaic attempts to uphold and reflect Catalan pluralism over the national question lacked the strength to prevent this polarization from infecting the party and threatened to descend into factionalism and division. By the time of the October referendum, CatComú was struggling to preserve its unity in the face of increasingly assertive internal currents of opinion – not envisaged in the party statutes – that were crystallizing over Catalonia's relationship to Spain.

Disunited Comuns

The Comuns-Podem saga had obscured the existence of other debates within CatComú itself that had not been resolved by the time of the founding assembly, which had left the definitive organizational and leadership structures to be decided the following year. An unfortunate consequence was that the new party was still self-preoccupied during 2018, despite the pressing need for it to grow beyond the metropolitan area and provide a convincing response to the challenge posed by the independence question. To many, the Comuns appeared to be playing for time in the hope that the independence issue would lose salience. Instead, the Catalan conflict imposed itself on the Comuns, threatening to undermine the confluence strategy and subvert the party construction process. CatComú's immediate horizons were set on the next round of elections, but normal politics had broken down. Widespread Catalan defiance of Spanish authority had been seen both in the referendum on 1 October, in which 2.3 million Catalan voters participated (42.3 per cent), with over 90 per cent voting yes to independence, and in the general strike and massive protest that took place two days later in reaction to the violent methods used by the Civil Guard and Spanish police in their attempt to prevent voting. An implicit declaration of independence on 10 October was then temporarily suspended in a move by Puigdemont to avert central state intervention and allow time for an attempt to obtain outside mediation, but after the majority in the Catalan Parliament had formally declared independence on 27 October, the Rajoy government made use of Article 155 of the Constitution to oust Puigdemont's government and call another Catalan election. Thus, the next regional election, in December, was the result of state imposition.

In these circumstances, Podem's executive called for a boycott of the event, only to trigger an intervention by the leadership of Podemos in November. This prompted Fachin along with one-third of Podem's Citizen Council members to abandon the party. Meanwhile, a majority within Podem (72 per cent in a consultation in which 60 per cent took part) voted to ally with CatComú in the election. 'CatComú-Podem' thus participated in the election, demanding rescission of Article 155, the release of imprisoned Catalan political leaders, a negotiated referendum and the return of a social agenda, seen as lacking during the independence challenge.

While CatComú-Podem relations now seemed to be mending, fissiparous tendencies developed among the Comuns themselves. Their denunciations of police behaviour in October and participation in protests about the 'repression' of the pro-sovereignty movement were viewed as excessive by their federalist wing which formalized its existence as *Comuns Federalistes*, in opposition to the independence process, in November. There was media speculation about growing dissatisfaction when CatComú-Podem's lists of candidates for the Catalan election were announced, following elite-level bargaining. The list headed by Domènech in Barcelona province included only two figures from ICV and one from EUiA, compared with four from BComú and three from Podem. However, CatComú's *inscritos* overwhelmingly approved its lists, by 674–34 votes, suggesting great confidence in the candidates chosen. Approval of the alliance with Podem was less emphatic (785–190).

A disappointing election result led to more questioning within CatComú. The new alliance won 40,000 votes less than CSQP had done in 2015 and only 8 seats (down 3) out of 135. Moreover, it continued to rely heavily on Barcelona (277,000 of its 326,000 votes) and came only fifth in both city and province. The remaining seats saw a 70–57 balance between independence and unionist forces, although the equation was complicated by the fact that the CUP now refused to support governments formed by the Puigdemont-led 'Junts per Catalunya' (JxCat) list and ERC, and by the inability of self-exiled and imprisoned pro-independence deputies to take up their seats in the Catalan Parliament. After months of impasse, with Puigdemont himself proving unable to secure presidential investiture, a minority government headed by Quim Torra, a pro-independence figure not facing prosecution, was formed in May 2018. CatComú-Podem voted against his investiture, but, unlike the unionist parties, was prepared to negotiate pragmatically with him, notably on budget proposals. De facto, despite its small number, it represented an arithmetically significant parliamentary group – one that would condemn Torra's government to roll forward the existing budget when attempts to persuade him to agree to a more socially ambitious new budget had failed. This did not translate into positive political influence for the alternative left, however. Prior to Torra's investiture, Domènech's proposal had suggested a way out of the parliamentary impasse, consisting of a broad-based government formed by independents whose agenda would simply be to restore Catalan autonomy and introduce emergency social measures, but had failed to win support.

Initially there was more effective collaboration within the new parliamentary group than there had been within CSQP (Albiach interview, 25 May 2018; Segovia interview, 11 April 2019) and CatComú-Podem relations improved too, partly because of Domènech's ability to stand above parties, his dual Podemos-Comuns affiliation and his close friendship with Iglesias. With the latter's endorsement, he decided to stand in the primary elections to decide Podem's new leadership in April, in what some circles saw as a 'hostile takeover bid' yet which he described as a way of bringing stability and ending the divide that had marred the birth of CatComú. Some 6,800 Podem supporters voted in these primaries in which there were five candidates. Domènech became secretary-general with 72 per cent of the votes, ahead of Noelia Bail, a former member of the Fachin executive, with 9 per cent. Both candidates favoured confluence, but the latter only through a continuing alliance or a party federation.

The difficulties were now located among the constituent elements of CatComú. On the eve of another party assembly in April 2018, its leadership faced criticism from the federalist current for concentrating on organizational questions rather than the recent electoral setback. An ICV conference in March had come out in favour of a more unequivocal federalist project and had been openly critical of the 'right to decide' formula that the Comuns had been united over in the past. The federalists criticized CatComú further for acquiring a 'vertical structure of leaderships and their teams' rather than relying on the 'collective strength of a horizontal democratic organization' (*El País*, 2 April 2018); their own ideas for building a rank-and-file structure defended the traditional model based on members with rights and duties plus a stable register of supporters. Some of the Comuns saw membership fees as essential for a solid grassroots organization to be built, whereas others (especially from BComú) saw them as a barrier to the building of a broad citizen base and defended CatComú's existing range of funding sources: parliamentary subsidies, salary contributions by elected officials and voluntary contributions.

The assembly itself adopted statutes, an ethical code and rules governing internal elections. CatComú's representational structures were now finalized: an Assembly based on the *inscritos* meeting biannually, a large National Council, a national Executive Committee of 30–40 members and a Coordination group of 2–4 people to carry out the decisions of the other bodies. All representative bodies and election lists were to be based on gender parity and alternation in lists; the *inscritos* would be organized at municipal level into local groups known as El Comú and there would also be a new territorial structure across Catalonia (*Europa Press*, 21 April 2018). Organized from above, the least convincing part of the design was that for the local structures. Pragmatically, it was recognized that BComú already had a consolidated functioning organizational model that it made sense to exempt from the new scheme. Thus, BComú would just coordinate with the new structure through a committee. The approach to other existing confluences in the metropolitan area was less clear, yet this was a crucial question with CatComú already needing to prepare for the municipal elections just a year away.

Ensuing elections to the new bodies brought out the contours of the new factionalism more clearly. Three lists were presented in June: (1) a transversal list incorporating people from different currents called *Construïm en Comú*, with Domènech and Colau as candidates for general co-coordinators; (2) *Comuns federalistes*, headed by former councillor José Luis Atienza; and (3) *Desbordem* led by ECP deputy Sònia Farré, based on Podem anti-capitalists who advocated breaking with Spain and defying its authority. The issue now was whether cooperation between the currents would be possible via the first of these lists, aiming at maintaining a balance between them, given that it was the likely winner. By June, there was considerable BComú and ICV questioning of the list negotiated by Domènech for giving pro-sovereignty elements too much prominence, although by no means all of these were separatists. Much of this criticism focused on the role of Alamany, who resigned as CatComú spokesperson in order to concentrate on being spokesperson for the parliamentary group.

The manifesto of the Domènech-Colau list emphasized municipalist commitment as the glue uniting the new party and avoided any positioning in the sovereignty debate, yet this remained an explosive issue, not least because minority lists winning at least 10 per cent of the votes qualified for representation on the new executive. The transversal list won 65.0 per cent of the votes to the Federalists' 21.1 per cent and Desbordem's 13.9 per cent in an election in which 35.9 per cent of CatComú's *inscritos* took part (3,620 out of 9,088, a drop of 2,000 in the numbers voting compared with the founding assembly). The new executive was formed by 20 members of the winning list and 6 and 4 respectively from the other lists. Domènech described its diversity as positive, but it brought paralysis when the new executive proceeded to the allocation of responsibilities. His surprise resignation on 4 September attracted further media attention to what was now becoming a party crisis. One reason given for his decision was sheer exhaustion, despite being just 43 years old: he had led the ECP group in the Congress of Deputies, then led CatComú and the parliamentary group, and more recently had become Podem leader as well. Other reasons were more to do with political frustration: the Comuns had not been able to open up a way forward for Catalonia, overcoming the impasse between the independence and unionist blocs; and the CatComú confluence was being subverted by internal political arguments over the national question, preventing it from becoming the 'empowered citizenry' it claimed to be (https://catalunyaencomu.cat/ca/qui-som), or even moving gradually in this direction. Domènech had not got his way in discussions over who would occupy key posts in the new leadership, his initial idea having been to have Alamany as a general coordinator. Resolving the Alamany controversy by eventually resorting to the far less controversial Colau did not address the underlying malaise.

Widely noted for political intelligence, charisma and ability to get on with a variety of political forces, Domènech was a huge loss to the Comuns. There was now a big, multiple political vacuum and Colau's authority was fully deployed in seeking a way to fill it. Her formula for the parliamentary group led to Albiach (Podem) becoming its leader while Alamany remained spokesperson, yet while Albiach counted with cross-party support, federalists saw Alamany, with her pro-sovereignty views, as unsuitable for the role of spokesperson. For the small coordinating body, Colau's proposal was a four-member team consisting of herself, another Comun and members of ICV and EUiA. There was some questioning of her nominations by independents on the CatComú executive and by EUiA, since they involved a person belonging to a *minority* faction within the latter, although proposed – like all nominees – for their individual merits. Eventual modifications, reducing the coordinating body to three, brought the assent of both executive and national committee for a design that, on the one hand, produced a more collective structure of leadership and, on the other, gave more weight to people close to Colau, including the key position of organization and territorial secretary to Susanna Segovia of BComú. This left some to claim that an inner core within BComú – essentially the 'Guanyem' network – was playing an excessive role in what was intended as a Catalan project, yet which they claimed was focused now too much on the re-election of the Colau administration. They expressed political misgivings about what they saw as Colau's desire to draw closer to ERC, in preparation for a future municipal coalition.

A month later, in October, CatComú divisions over the national question deepened when members of the pro-sovereignty current, headed by Nuet and Alamany, established a new platform, *Sobiranistes*. After January, when the party's national council passed a resolution calling for a negotiated solution to the national question, the platform claimed that this was a retreat from the founding document, which had envisaged sovereignty being won through constituent processes in Catalonia and in Spain; moreover, CatComú was failing to measure up to confluence ideals, operating instead through elitist backroom negotiations among the component party leaderships, which was driving away members (Sobiranistes, 2018; Alamany interview, 10 April 2019; Nuet interview in *Cuarto Poder*, 20 March 2019). Alamany blamed the paralysis of the CatComú project on ICV, but implied that centralizing dynamics emanating from BComú were also problematic, at odds with the original values of the project; the parties needed to take a step back. After resisting the sacking of Marc Grau as coordinator of the parliamentary group, she resigned as spokesperson. In February 2019, she went on to abandon the group while retaining her seat, an act viewed by the Comuns as deeply contrary to the principle of common ownership of representation; they criticized her too for not raising her criticisms internally before deciding to jump ship. By this time, she and Nuet were heading towards collaborating with ERC in the municipal and general elections of 2019, respectively, in competition with the Comuns. While personal dissatisfaction over the recent personnel changes in the CatComú leadership was certainly one motivation here, their political discourse held that the October referendum had created a new context for Catalonia in which left-wing pro-sovereignty groups needed to reposition themselves closer to the independence forces (Alamany interview, 10 April 2019; Segovia interview, 11 April 2019). Although they took very few CatComú members with them, their departure gave the impression that the Comuns were being torn apart by the national question.

Less than two years after its foundation, Cat Comú was a project enveloped in crises and it was still only in an alliance with Podem, in which primaries had given rise to a new executive led by Bail in November 2018, just five months after the previous ones. As a project of transcendence, it certainly had a long way to go. As the elections of 2019 drew near, it was clear that diverse expressions of the alternative left would be presented to voters through a variety of lists across Catalonia, appearing as CatComú in some places, as alliances of some of its political components elsewhere or as local municipalist citizen platforms, some of them grouped in a rival confluence project involving the

CUP (Candidatura d'Unitat Popular (Popular Unity Candidature), members of the Comuns belonging to the pro-sovereignty sector and independents. This, together with the special organizational status that BComú enjoyed in relation to CatComú, suggested that the new party would be unable to apply a general electoral strategy throughout Catalonia. During 2018 the party had been looking to make gains primarily in the metropolitan area in the municipal elections the following May. Its planning had to be rethought in February 2019 when Pedro Sánchez called an early general election for 28 April 2019.

It is questionable whether CatComú can remedy its weaknesses through modifications made by its leaders. In 2019, it would prove robust enough for its different political families to collaborate in the election campaigns; people with different positions on the national question worked well together and nobody raised issues about the head of the general election list, Jaume Asens, being a sovereignty advocate (Salado interview, 9 April 2019). Yet there was clearly a strong tension between the 'top-down' nature of the Catalan party's design and construction and the municipalist experience of BComú, as well as major questions over whether the participative and feminist practices of the latter could be translated to the Catalan level, not least because of the difference of scale. CatComú lacked the extensive participative process that characterized BComú's preparation of its programme for the European elections and its election campaign committee was largely composed of men. The more vertical organizational structure of the Catalan party, undertaken with a confluence perspective but without the horizontality and social movement input that had characterized BComú, inevitably involved some persistence of the old-style politics (Lo Cascio interview, 8 April 2019; Shea Baird interview, 12 April 2019). Domènech may have been thinking partly along these lines when he observed that Catalunya en Comú was not in fact an example of 'new politics' whereas the case of BComú was somewhat different (Domènech 2016: 73).

7 Consolidation and prospects

The Comuns managed to form a second government in Barcelona following the municipal election in May 2019. However, this was a year that brought major electoral disappointments for them. Both they and Podemos suffered setbacks in the general election on 28 April 2019 and lost ground in the municipal and European elections on 26 May 2019. In the municipal elections, while recording poor results elsewhere in Catalonia, in the city of Barcelona the Comuns emerged from a desperately close contest less than 5,000 votes behind the Left Republicans. Ada Colau recognized their defeat ... yet by mid-June BComú was back in office as a result of coalition negotiations and the decision by three independents associated with the new unionist Barcelona pel Canvi (BCN Canvi) platform, headed by Manuel Valls to vote for the investiture of Colau, rather than allow the pro-independence ERC (Esquerra Republicana de Catalunya, Republican Left of Catalonia) candidate, Ernest Maragall (brother of Pasqual) to become mayor. With support forthcoming from a strengthened PSC, once again seen as a potential coalition partner, BComú was thus given an opportunity to consolidate the policy changes already underway.

The first section of this concluding chapter examines these electoral contests for the light they shed on the Comuns' political standing, through BComú and CatComú. It also discusses the outcome of the elections for their coalition implications in Barcelona, since in the context of persisting party system fragmentation, the Comuns will need to collaborate with other parties now more than previously if they are to achieve majorities on the city council. The second section of the chapter then identifies some of the organizational development questions they face moving forward. The two parts cohere because the elections provided evidence that, at least judged by conventional standards, the Comuns remain organizationally weak. Certain debates now need more urgent resolution. Catalunya en Comú has developed with significant differences to the original model of BComú. The tensions between them have become evident and could even lead to a contest over which model will prevail.

From electoral disappointments to a second Colau administration

The general election on 28 April 2019 showed the Comuns to be losing ground as some of their erstwhile voters switched to the PSC (Partit dels Socialistes de Catalunya, Socialist Party of Catalonia). This was an important Spanish contest in which Pedro Sánchez and the PSOE (Partido Socialista Obrero Español, Spanish Socialist Workers' Party) were seen as the best bet to defeat a challenge from three forces on the right: PP (Partido Popular, People's Party), Cs (Ciudadanos, Citizens) and now the far right Vox as well, which had been cooperating to take control of political institutions since the regional elections in Andalucía the previous December. Benefitting from tactical voting, the PSOE boosted its representation in Congress from 85 to 123 seats, although primarily at the expense of its main potential governmental partner, UP (its name now rendered in the feminine form as *Unidas Podemos*). Having displayed marked disunity in places such as Madrid and Galicia, UP's tally dropped from 71 to 42 seats. The Comuns' ECP-Guanyem el Canvi list, headed by Asens (and with Pisarello presented in third place), had a programme offering more feminism, democracy, social justice, sovereignty and climate justice (Catalunya en Comú, 2019). Their representation fell from 12 to 7, by losing the two seats they had held in the provinces of Girona and Lleida and dropping from 9 to 6 in Barcelona, while hanging on to their one seat in Tarragona. Overall, the Comuns lost 240,000 votes across Catalonia and ended up on 14.9 per cent, well behind an ERC-Sobiranistes list on 24.6 per cent and the PSC on 23.2 per cent. On a higher turnout, in an election overshadowed by the ongoing trial of the 12 imprisoned independence leaders in Madrid (among them ERC leader Junqueras, who headed its electoral list), the Left Republicans made gains, chiefly at the expense of JxCat, and won their first ever general election victory in Catalonia.

Although CatComú had been prioritizing Colau's re-election as mayor and the Comuns' setback was expected, the results in Barcelona were particularly disappointing: a bad omen for the municipal elections taking place just four weeks later. The Socialists won in all the big cities of the province except for Barcelona itself while ERC-Sobiranistes triumphed there. In the city, ECP lost 53,000 votes, dropping from 25.7 per cent to 16.3 per cent. ERC and the PSC increased their votes in every single *barrio* whereas ECP fell back everywhere, winning in only two of the 73 *barrios*. Of course, different dynamics would be involved in the May elections, but it was clear that both ERC and the Socialists were on a roll and likely to make further gains. This was also ERC's first ever victory in the city.

While the municipal elections were deemed key to its future, Barclona en Comú also put considerable effort into preparing for the contemporaneous European elections, seeing them as an opportunity to take its radical municipalist voice into the European Parliament (EP). It organized six public debates to develop ideas for its programme and held workshops with MEPs and representatives from reformist local governments in other parts of Spain. The proposals were discussed extensively in BComú policy groups and neighbourhood assemblies and were finalized by its plenary. However, its idea of trying to earmark a place on UP's European electoral list for a specifically municipalist candidate, to be negotiated with the Comuns' partners therein, was seen by many in CatComú as anathema: as evidence that BComú was losing enthusiasm for the Catalan confluence project. In the end, following a tense argument, negotiations in Madrid resulted in Barcelona en Comú's candidate only being allocated twelfth position on the 'Unidas Podemos Cambiar Europa' (United We Can Change Europe) list which, with UP doing badly in opinion polls, was expected to lose some of the 11 seats won by equivalent forces five years earlier. In the event, the Spanish alternative left's representation dropped to six seats in the May election, with Ernest Urtasan of CatComú remaining the sole MEP from the Comuns component of the UP contingent within the European United Left-Nordic Green Left parliamentary group of the EP. Earlier, some 3,274 Catalunya en Comú *inscritos* had taken part in an Internet-based primary (won by Urtasan) and consultation about participating in the UP list.

One development that gave the Comuns hope of repeating their 2015 victory in the municipal election was a resurgent rivalry between JxCat and ERC, notwithstanding their ongoing collaboration in the Torra government. They presented different lists for the EP elections, in which, with the exception of the city of Barcelona, the Junts list headed by Puigdemont, with 4.6 per cent of the vote and two seats, was outpolled by the ERC-led Ahora Repúblicas (Republics Now) list headed by Junqueras, with 5.6 per cent and three seats. The tactic of selecting leading independence figures who were in prison or in Brussels was used by Junts also in the municipal election in Barcelona. Headed by the imprisoned Joaquim Forn, its list incorporated the PDeCAT but not the other pro-independence forces. Indeed, there were no less than four pro-independence lists presented in the city, two of which (including the CUP) failed to reach the 5 per cent threshold for representation.

Despite the disunity of the independence parties, the Catalan situation weighed more heavily in this compared with the 2015 municipal elections, not least because the trials of the independence leaders were now at an advanced stage. Although the Comuns continued to demonstrate their solidarity with the prisoners, this emotive issue received more emphasis from ERC. There was also a bandwagon effect from the Socialist and ERC successes in the recent general election. Faced with these influences, the Comuns relied on their record in office as the key to re-election. Their electoral programme in Barcelona – again, the result of an extensive participative process – was devoted entirely to the changes BComú wished to press ahead with in the city, including several measures that had been blocked thus far (water remunicipalization, the tram link and a public funeral company). The most notable novelty was a pledge to boost police numbers by 1,000, of which 600 were envisaged to be Mossos (demanded by BComú from the Generalitat) and 400 Guardia Urbana (Barcelona en Comú, 2019: 19). Colau herself reiterated the Comuns' support for a Catalan republic but maintained that Barcelona needed an eminently municipal project and that this was what the election should focus upon.

Following media criticism for having used a non-competitive 'primary' in 2015 – in effect, a vote to endorse a closed list drawn up through negotiation between component parties – BComú debated whether to adopt a different approach to the 2019 election. Since Colau's own candidacy was unquestioned, nobody saw any point in staging what would be an artificial contest. The issue was how to compose the remainder of the list. In the name of producing a cohesive team, able to govern, the mayor's proposal was that she be allowed to compose her own list once the criteria for selection had been agreed upon in a democratic manner. The alternative considered was to have a competitive primary for the remainder of the list, which would then be constituted proportionally to reflect the voting. In the end, Colau's proposal found favour, the mainstream view being that the business of selecting a list whose aspiration was to govern a city was different from the task of preparing a list for an election about parliamentary representation. Another difference in the Comuns' methodology this time, reflecting the progression of the confluence process, was that it was no longer the support of a component political party that candidates needed in order to be considered for the list but rather the support of at least two local assemblies or an assembly plus a policy group (Forné interview, 8 April 2019; Shea Baird interview, 12 April 2019).

Seeing the mobilization of supporters as crucial to the outcome of the contest with ERC, the Comuns for the first time used door-to-door canvassing in the poorer *barrios* that had supported them in the past.

They had brought in trainers from the Working Families Party of the USA for guidance on how to do this and one point learnt was the importance of developing a diversity agenda in order to broaden their base, ethnic minorities having been a rather neglected focus thus far. This, together with the introduction of new procedures for integrating new recruits, including regular welcome meetings, boosted BComú activist numbers from 1,500 to 3,000 during the final year of their term, most of them joining in the early months of 2019 (Shea Bird interview, 12 April 2019). Beyond Barcelona, meanwhile, the organizational weakness of the Comuns was much more evident. Whereas ERC was able to present lists in 807 municipalities across Catalonia, CatComú as such was only present in 151 and it was allied with Podem in just some 20 places (Segovia interview, 11 April 2019).

Election day on 26 May 2019 saw a rise in turnout of 6 per cent. Table 7.1 presents the end result. The narrow defeat for the Comuns came not so much from direct competition from ERC, which attracted part of the former Convergència vote, but rather BComú's loss of the district of Nou Barris to the PSC, as support dropped there from 33 per cent to 23 per cent. Despite winning in six of the ten districts, the Comuns' vote was down most markedly in the poorer ones (Nou Barris, Sant Andreu and Sant Martí) while across the city it fell by one-fifth (from 25.2 per cent to 20.7 per cent). The only satisfying feature was a comfortable victory in Ciutat Vella (27.5 per cent), where BComú's relatively good performance in El Raval (28.1 per cent) suggested that the criticism of the Colau administration for inadequate responses to common crime, drug-trafficking and prostitution was by no means universally held.

Table 7.1 Results of the municipal election in Barcelona, 2019

Party*	Votes	% of valid votes	Seats	Variation 2015
ERC	160,990	21.4	10	+5
BComú	156,157	20.7	10	-1
PSC	138,748	18.4	8	+4
BCN Canvi-Cs	99,494	13.2	6	+1**
Junts	78,957	10.5	5	-5***
PP	37,745	5.0	2	-1

Source: Ajuntament de Barcelona, available at : www.bcn.cat/estadistica/angles/dades/telec/loc/loc19/t33.htm

Note: *including allies; **compared with Cs alone; ***compared with CiU.

Beyond the city, the panorama facing the Comuns was no better. In the metropolitan area of Barcelona, the Socialists triumphed by winning back part of the vote lost to confluences in 2015. The Comuns led in 13 municipalities won by ICV-EUiA four years earlier, but lost control of another dozen; dropping from 18.4 per cent to 15.7 per cent of the vote, they came only third in the AMB overall, behind the PSC and ERC. In the province of Barcelona, where the PSC also won, the Comuns came fourth, behind Junts, while across the whole of Catalonia, ERC moved up from third to first (3,107 councillors), followed by the Socialists, Junts and the Comuns (258). Elsewhere in Spain too, there were several blows for the alternative left, most crucially in Madrid, where a divided left found itself facing an overall right-wing majority for the PP, Cs and Vox; better news was restricted largely to Valencia and Cádiz, where 'mayors for change' were again returned to office.

Faced with the results in Barcelona, Colau congratulated Maragall on his victory, pointed to the arithmetic of a potential 28-seat majority for the combined forces of the left and urged him to negotiate an ERC-BComú-PSC tripartite coalition committed to a municipal agenda, rather than look to Junts and the Comuns for a pro-sovereignty majority. In fact, both formulas were problematic: ERC and the PSC ruled out collaboration with each other, as did Junts and the Comuns. The independence forces were still aiming to commit the city to the Catalan process, but their combined representation had dropped from 18 to 15 seats and Junts had suffered huge losses to ERC. The governmental outcome was thus extremely uncertain … at least until 29 May, when Valls declared that he was willing to lend his group's support to the investiture of Colau, without asking anything in return, in order to prevent an independence advocate (Maragall) becoming mayor. This turn of events made feasible the idea of another BComú-PSC minority coalition, although Colau – not wanting to be associated with the unionist Valls – continued to call for a *tripartito*. It left the Comuns with the decision of whether to present Colau for investiture, for which she needed an absolute majority of 21, or allow Maragall to be elected on a second investiture vote, as candidate of the party with the most votes.

This was a difficult decision for the Comuns. Although part of BComú was not keen on joining forces with the PSC again, this was not a problem for many others, citing the relative ranking of the parties and their proximity on many municipal issues. To receive votes from Valls, however, would tarnish the image of the Comuns and antagonize ERC, who would feel that their victory had been stolen from them. At the same time, much was at stake: the chance to complete BComú's municipal agenda and the desire to avoid an organizational crisis which either collaboration with Maragall or opposition status threatened to bring, Barcelona's city hall being the only major institution the Comuns controlled. Some well-attended BComú district assemblies discussed three formulas: (1) the tripartite formula; (2) governing with ERC; or (3) governing with the PSC, the last of these options being increasingly prioritized by Colau. This was for Barcelona alone, not as a macro-strategy for Catalonia. Basing their coalition decisions on local circumstances, the Comuns meanwhile helped ERC candidates take mayoral positions from PSC incumbents in Tarragona and Lleida.

BComú's coordinating body met early in June and backed the idea of Colau presenting her candidature. This position was hugely supported in an ensuing plenary, by 457–27 votes (94.4 per cent). The aim was still eventually to negotiate a tripartite coalition, but it was clear that there was no possibility of this happening any time soon, for it would require both ERC and PSC to rethink their positions. Instead, agreement was reached with the Socialists to negotiate a bilateral coalition after the investiture vote on 15 June. The PSC's modest preconditions for backing Colau were that BComú's leadership should indicate its preference for the Socialists over ERC and that its supporters should vote on which party they preferred as a coalition partner. BComú's statutes in any case gave the final word to its 9,949 *inscritos*, some 40 per cent of whom voted in the ensuing consultation, 71.4 per cent for a coalition with the PSC and 28.6 per cent to go with ERC. At a very late stage in the talks, Maragall had proposed sharing the mayoral term with Colau but had not reconsidered his pledge to press for another independence referendum.

In the investiture session, Colau proceeded to receive 21 votes (BComú, PSC and the three from BCN Canvi) while Maragall received 15 (ERC and Junts). BComú was thus returned to office, although not in the way the Comuns wanted. Their readiness to use BCN Canvi votes was criticized by DiEM25, the European movement led by Yanis Varoufakis. And far from the festive atmosphere that had surrounded Colau's investiture four years earlier, this time the Plaça Sant Jaume was filled with more angry pro-independence protestors than BComú supporters and the female leaders of the new administration faced a barrage of thrown objects and *machista* abuse from a sector of the crowd as they crossed the square to make the customary courtesy visit to the president of the Generalitat. Many other protesters simply demanded the release of Joaquim Forn, who had been brought to the ceremony from prison, and was returned there afterwards. The Comuns would share the posts in the new metropolitan government with the PSC, ERC and JxCat.

At the municipal level, the new balance of forces led the Comuns to make more significant policy concessions to the Socialists as well as concede a larger share of the political appointments than during the first coalition, as the price paid to secure stable government of the city and a reinforcement of policy initiatives at the metropolitan level. The coalition agreement eventually announced on 10 July allocated some significant portfolios to the Socialists, including security, mobility and economic promotion of the city (which went to Collboni, who also became principal deputy mayor), while the Comuns remained in charge of the budget, urban planning, social services, housing and culture. The only clear policy fundamental of the Comuns to be questioned by the Socialists was the plan to remunicipalize water services, a measure that was still being challenged through the courts by the existing provider, Agbar. The parties to the pact agreed a *modus operandi* to manage their differences over Catalan assertions of sovereignty, each being left free to express their own viewpoints while committing jointly to the principle that the government of Barcelona should not be subordinated to any extra-municipal 'logic, criterion or institution' in this respect. Now that the immediate round of elections was over, Colau returned a yellow ribbon insignia to the balcony of city hall, but only after putting the matter to a vote on the committee formed by municipal party spokespersons. In this way her new administration reaffirmed the Comuns' solidarity with the 12 imprisoned independence leaders as they awaited sentence by Spain's Supreme Court. Yet it seemed likely that for the Comuns in this administration, sovereignty would be more a statement of constitutional preference than a fundamental basis for future action. Barcelona en Comú would maintain a crucial distinction between what it wanted to do in the city and its support for a republic: the former being in the municipal domain, the latter a Catalan matter.

Ongoing debates and international significance

Apart from the difficulties of a minority administration that would still need to work hard for majority support on Barcelona's city council, the Comuns also faced questions about their own organizational model following their run of disappointing election results. Some issues were already subject to ongoing debate while others had yet to be confronted. Now there seemed more urgency, not least because of the financial consequences of poor election results: prior to the 2019 elections, BComú had been reliant on parliamentary subsidies earned through ECP for roughly half its income (Shea Baird interview, 12 April 2019).

Today, there are at least four major questions that the Comuns face at the organizational level. First, there is a discussion in BComú over whether it should seek to develop further as a movement that intervenes in political life or as a party committed to participative democracy. People who joined the Comuns via a political party tend to argue for greater commitment and discipline as standards for membership; others point to the advantages of the existing, more relaxed regime if people with demanding family or work commitments are to be retained and new people attracted. Even if the current hybrid model of BComú remains the compromise favoured by a majority, there will still be specific issues to address regarding funding of the organization and the role of the less active members, the *inscritos*. Apart from online decision-making votes, the statutes envisage the latter participating in an annual assembly, yet uncertainty over its purpose first led the event to be postponed and then, when eventually held in 2019, it was a very poorly attended affair, the agenda announcing it having offered little more than an opportunity to show approval of the municipal electoral list.

Second, with the Comuns only just gaining a second term of office, there is the linked issue of how to grow and renew the membership. This has not been a constant priority for the Comuns thus far, but now seems destined to become one. Ada Colau herself has indicated that this will very likely to be her last term as mayor and the same applies to all Comuns representatives and officials once they have served the normal maximum of two terms stipulated in their statutes. On membership, one question is whether it is enough just to mobilize supporters as key elections draw near. Arguably, BComú might have been able to push through a popular plan, such as the tram link, when it was blocked by opposition parties, if it had been able to develop more of a presence on the ground. There is also the challenge of expanding the socio-economic and demographic composition of the membership. The question of ethnic diversity was tabled rather late in the day, as mentioned above. Rejuvenation of the organization has not been addressed vigorously at all, yet this is important both electorally and existentially. The age profile reported to a BComú plenary in March 2018 showed that, while the thirties and forties cohorts represented 32 per cent of activists and 52 per cent of *inscritos* and the age 50+ cohort represented 37 per cent and 28 per cent, the under-30s were only 5 per cent of the activists (less than the general demographic distribution) and 9 per cent of *inscritos* (Barcelona en Comú, 2018: 11).

Third, there is the question of the relationship between BComú and CatComú, two rather different organizations as things stand. Within the latter, some believe that the coordination mechanisms are defective and are not delivering harmony between the two organizations; they want BComú to become more integrated with the Catalan party. Others see this idea as problematic and fear that a lot of what is truly innovative and valuable about Barcelona en Comú would be lost in the process. They refer to the way in which the internal divisions that have tested CatComú coherence over sovereignty issues eventually tended to be replicated in BComú in votes to decide its strategic approach to the EP elections of 2019; those associated with currents within CatComú tended to vote *en bloc* if they were active also in BComú. Moreover, besides the relationship between the Barcelona and Catalan organizations of the Comuns, there are related questions about how Barcelona en Comú might seek to improve its relations with other confluences within the metropolitan area and CatComú with other expressions of the alternative left, including Podem, across Catalonia.

Fourth, following the poor showing of the Comuns in the municipal elections, and with their strategic position in Barcelona now looming even larger within their political constellation, there may be a need to give more thought to what can be achieved by radical citizen-based platforms in smaller municipalities that lack the critical mass and resources of the prosperous Catalan capital. BComú has tended to present its *municipalista* badge of identity as self-explanatory and has had little to say about differences in scale across municipalities. It may be that its participative processes can be made to work across a range of localities, up to city scale, but inevitably the potential for municipal administrations councils to address issues of social inequality must vary greatly.

How (and whether) the Comuns address these questions will be studied not only by conventional parties, media commentators and academic observers but by other organizations of the alternative left elsewhere. For many, the evolution of BComú and CatComú will continue to be of interest in relation to what can be achieved through electoral interventions by the alternative left and citizen-based platforms in the name of pursuing a more participative democracy and social transformations, with special interest existing around the feminization agenda, the attempt to manage mass tourism and responses to the deepening environmental challenge. Meanwhile, the challenge posed to the Comuns by Catalonia's national question could well become a point of reference for the left in countries where it needs to define itself in relation to popular movements seeking independence for non-sovereign regions forming part of larger states.

The Comuns are already seen as a model by a number of like-minded movements and parties in places where social movements and radical left groups are seeking to intervene in local political institutions for the first time, or where left-wing forces are attempting to unite and create something new that goes beyond the limits of an alliance or coalition. Confluence politics have clearly enjoyed some degree of success in Barcelona itself, but can make fewer claims in respect of Catalonia as a whole and have ended in more resounding failure in some other parts of Spain. In fact, what has been done in its name provides a series of 'models' that can be found in different parts of Spain, with Catalonia offering a particularly sharp contrast in nature between the two organizations promoted by the Comuns. Such models are useful pedagogically only if they are used critically to extract lessons. They cannot simply be followed or implemented by movements elsewhere without considering specificities of context, which will always be different in some respects. In particular, the question of the geopolitical scale on which certain practices, especially participative practices, can prosper has been suggested to be crucial in the pages of this book. Following César Rendueles, one must play the 'devil's advocate' and ask whether participative democracy projects may not be harder to develop above the municipal level in the mass societies of the early twenty-first century (Subirats and Rendueles, 2016: 14–16); but one must also question whether the Barcelona en Comú model is relevant to municipalities in general, or largely just to major global cities such as Barcelona. If so, in the Catalan context, its effectiveness will continue to be a fact chiefly in the city of Barcelona and possibly in the wider metropolitan area. To achieve more, across Catalonia, would mean going beyond the well-established historical pattern of territorial unevenness that has long been problematic for the Catalan Left.

Appendix: List of interviews

Positions indicated are those held at time of interview.

Elisenda Alamany, former Catalunya en Comú-Podem member of the Catalan Parliament, 10 April 2019.

Jéssica Albiach, leader of Catalunya en Comú-Podem group, Catalan Parliament, 25 May 2018.

Antonio Balmón, PSC-PSOE, mayor of Cornellà de Llobregat, 3 April 2017.

Alfred Bosch, leader of ERC group on city council, 12 November 2016.

Jaume Bosch, ICV-EUiA, member of the Catalan Parliament, 11 February 2014.

Miriam Casals, (with Jordi Garbarró), president of Òmnium Cultural, 12 February 2014.

Ferran Caymel, adviser to BComú municipal group in Ciutat Vella, 7 April 2017.

David Cid, national coordinator of ICV, 9 November 2016.

Sergi de Maya, ICV/BComú, member of social rights team, Ajuntament de Barcelona, 3 April 2017.

Xavi Farré, BComú district councillor, Sants-Montjuïch, 23 May 2018.

David Fernàndez, CUP, former member of the Catalan Parliament, 6 April 2017.

Carme Forcadell, president of the Assemblea Nacional Catalana, 26 November 2013.

Laia Forné, Barcelona en Comú, policy advisor, Regidoria de Participació i Territori, Ajuntament de Barcelona, 8 April 2019.

Ricard Gomà, ICV/BComú member, 11 November 2016.

Paola Lo Cascio, Catalunya en Comú executive member (2017–2018), 22 May 2018, 8 April 2019.

Ernest Maragall, Nova Esquerra Catalana leader, 10 February 2014.

Jordi Martín López, BComú district councillor, Sant Martí, 23 May 2018.

Jordi Mir Garcia, social scientist, Universitat Pompeu Fabra, 8 April 2017, 24 May 2018.

Joan Josep Nuet, EUiA/Catalunya en Comú-Podem, member of the Catalan Parliament, 6 April 2017.

Ferran Pedret, PSC-PSOE, member of the Catalan Parliament, 10 November 2016.

Laura Pérez, secretary-general of Podem in Barcelona, head of feminism and LGTBI department in city hall, 12 April 2019.

Marc Pradel Miquel, Universitat de Barcelona, sociologist, 6 April 2017.

Laura Roth, BComú, member of the international group, 8 November 2016.

Maria Rovira, CUP, Barcelona city councillor, 9 November 2016.

Toni Salado, EUiA/BComú, Diputació de Barcelona, 11 November 2016, 9 April 2019.

Susanna Segovia, Catalunya en Comú-Podem member of the Catalan Parliament, 11 April 2019.

Kate Shea Baird, BComú, executive member, 21 May 2018, 12 April 2019.

Miquel Strubell, Assemblea Nacional Catalana (founding member), 5 April 2017, 22 May 2018.

Joan Subirats, BComú, comissionat de Cultura, Ajuntament de Barcelona, 2018–19, 7 April 2017.

Xavier Trias, leader of CiU/PDeCAT group on city council, 8 November 2016.

Bibliography

Antentas, Josep Maria and Vivas, Esther (2011). La rebelión de l@s indignad@s. In Carlos Taibo, Josep Maria Antentas, Esther Vivas, et al. (eds), *La rebelión de los indignados*. Madrid: Popular.

Balfour, Sebastian (1989). *Dictatorship, Workers and the City: Labour in Greater Barcelona Since 1929*. Oxford: Clarendon.

Barcelona en Comú (2015). Programa electoral, municipales 2015. Available at: https://barcelonaencomu.cat/sites/default/files/programaencomun_cast.pdf (accessed 23 April 2015).

Barcelona en Comú (2017). Una organizació feminista i radicalment democràtica: Reflexions sobre la diagnosi de gènere. Available at: https://barcelona encomu.cat/.../files/document/informe-diagnosi-genere (accessed 30 May 2018).

Barcelona en Comú (2018). Pla d'acció 2018–2019 de Barcelona en Comú. Tenim més poder del que ens han fet creure. Approved 3 March. Available at: https:// barcelonaencomu.cat/sites/default/files/document/pla_daccio_bcomu_2018-19. pdf (accessed 10 October 2018).

Barcelona en Comú (2019). Plans per una Barcelona Futura. Programa electoral 2019–2023. Available at: https://barcelonaencomu.cat/sites/default/files/ document/bcomu_programa_.pdf (accessed 18 August 2019).

Boylan, Brendon M. (2015). In pursuit of independence: the political economy of Catalonia's secessionist movement. *Nations and Nationalism*, 21(4): 761–785.

Catalunya en Comú (2019). Guanyem per Avançar. Programa electoral, En Comú Podem. Available at: https://encomupodem.cat/programa-electoral (accessed 10 April 2019).

Colau, Ada (2015). First we take Barcelona… *Open Democracy*, 20 May. Available at: www.opendemocracy.net/en/can-europe-make-it/first-we-take-ba rcelona/ (accessed 25 May 2015).

Colau, Ada and Alemany, Adrià (2012). *Vidas hipotecadas*. Barcelona: Angle.

Colau, Ada and Alemany, Adrià (2013). *Sí que es pot! Crònica d'una petita gran victòria*. Barcelona: Destino.

Crameri, Kathryn (2014). *"Goodbye Spain?" The Question of Independence for Catalonia*. Brighton: Sussex Academic Press/Cañada Blanch.

Crameri, Kathryn (2015). Political power and civilian counterpower: the complex dynamics of the Catalan independence movement. *Nationalism and Ethnic Politics*, 21(1): 104–120.

Culla, Juan B. (2017). *El tsunami: Com i per qué el sistema de partits català ha esdevingut irreconeixible*. Barcelona: Pòrtic.

De Weert, J. and García, M. (2015). Housing crisis: the Platform of Mortgage Victims (PAH) movement in Barcelona and innovations in governance. *Journal of Housing and the Built Environment*, 31(3): 471–493.

Domènech, Xavier (2016). Interviewed by Sergi Picazo. In *Camins per l'hegemonia: Pensant històricament el present i el futur de Catalunya*. Barcelona: Icaria.

Dowling, Andrew (2018). *The Rise of Catalan Independence: Spain's Territorial Crisis*. Abingdon: Routledge.

Eizaguirre, Santiago, Pradel-Miquel, Marc and García, Marisol (2017). Citizenship practices and democratic governance: 'Barcelona en Comú' as an urban citizenship confluence promoting a new policy agenda. *Citizenship Studies*, 21(4): 425–439.

Fernàndez, David and de Jòdar, Julià (2016). *CUP: Viaje a las raíces y razones de las Candidaturas de Unidad Popular*. Madrid: Capitán Swing.

Garcia, Beatriz (2017). New citizenship in Spain: from social cooperation to self-government. *Citizenship Studies*, 21/(4): 455–467.

Gillespie, Richard (2017a). The contrasting fortunes of pro-sovereignty currents in Basque and Catalan nationalist parties: PNV and CDC compared. *Territory, Politics, Governance*, 5(4): 406–424.

Gillespie, Richard (2017b). Spain: the forward march of Podemos halted? *Mediterranean Politics*, 22(4): 537–544.

González-Enríquez, Carmen (2017). The Spanish exception: unemployment, inequality and immigration, but no right-wing populist parties. Working paper 3/2–17. Madrid: Real Instituto Elcano.

Guanyem Barcelona (2014). Manifest Guanyem Barcelona. Available at: https://barcelonaencomu.cat/ca/manifest-guanyem-barcelona (accessed 26 July 2015).

Guibernau, Montserrat (2014). Prospects for an Independent Catalonia. *International Journal of Politics, Culture, and Society*, 27(1): 5–23.

Laval, Christian and Dardot, Pierre (2015). *Común: Ensayo sobre revolución en el siglo XXI*. Barcelona: Gedisa; translation of *Commun*. Paris: La Découverte, 2014.

Magone, José M. (2018). *Contemporary Spanish Politics*, 3rd edn. Abingdon: Routledge.

Mota, Fabiola and Subirats, Joan (2002). Capital social et capacité de gouvernement politique: leurs effets sur la satisfaction et le soutien au système politique autonomique espagnol. *Pôle Sud*, 16: 107–124.

Muro, Diego (2015). When do countries recentralize? Ideology and party politics in the age of austerity. *Nationalism and Ethnic Politics*, 21(1): 24–43.

Observatorio Metropolitano (2014). *La apuesta municipalista: La democracia empieza por lo cercano*. Madrid: Traficantes de Sueños.

Pradel-Miquel, Marc (2016). *Catalunya, xarxa de ciutats: El municipalisme de Pasqual Maragall i la seva influència en la governança de Catalunya.* Barcelona: Fundació Catalunya Europa.

Real Instituto Elcano (2017). El proceso independentista catalàn: ¿cómo hemos llegado hasta aquí?, ¿cuál es su dimensión europea? ¿y qué puede ocurrir? Madrid: Real Instituto Elcano, 23 October.

Roller, Elisa and Van Houten, Pieter (2003). A national party in a regional party system: the PSC-PSOE in Catalonia. *Regional & Federal Studies*, 13(3): 1–22.

Russo Spena, Giacomo and Forti, Steven (2016). *Ada Colau, la città in comune.* Rome: Alegre.

Serra Carné, Joan (2016). *Ada, la rebel·lió democràtica.* Barcelona: Ara.

Serra Carné, Joan and González, Sara (2017). *El part dels Comuns: Relat del Naixement de Catalunya en Comú.* Barcelona: Saldonar.

Serrano, Ivan (2013). Just a matter of identity? Support for independence in Catalonia. *Regional and Federal Studies*, 23(5): 523–545.

Shea Baird, Kate (2015). Beyond Ada Colau: the common people in Barcelona en Comú. *Open Democracy*, 27 May. Available at: www.opendemocracy.net/ en/can-europe-make-it/beyond-ada-colau-common-people-of-barcelona-en-c omu/ (accessed 6 June 2015).

Shea Baird, Kate (2017). A new municipalist movement is on the rise—from small victories to global alternatives. *Open Democracy*, 7 June. Available at: www.opendemocracy.net/en/can-europe-make-it/new-international-municipa list-movement-is-on-rise-from-small-vic/ (accessed 8 July 2017).

Sobiranistes (2018). Un nou futur en comú, 23 October. Available at: www. sobiranistes.cat.

Stobart, Luke (2018). Why Podemos and els Comuns have so far failed the Catalan fight. *The Ecologist*, 30 May.

Subirats, Joan (2011). *Otra sociedad, ¿otra política? De "no nos representan" a la democracia de lo común.* Barcelona: Icaria.

Subirats, Joan and Rendueles, César (2016). *Los (bienes) comunes. ¿Oportunidad o espejismo?* Barcelona: Icaria.

Taibo, Carlos, Antentas, Josep Maria, Vivas, Esther, et al. (2011). *La rebelión de los indignados.* Madrid: Popular.

Tomàs Fornés, Mariona (2017). *Governar la Barcelona real: Pasqual Maragall i el dret a la ciutat metropolitana.* Barcelona: Fundació Catalunya Europa.

Tugas, Roger (2014). *Escac al poder: L'auge de l'esquerra alternativa.* Barcelona: Deu i Onze.

Un País en Comú (2017). Ideari politic i model de país. Available at: https:// unpaisencomu.cat/ideari-politic (accessed 20 April 2017).

Zechner, Manuela (2015). Barcelona en Comú: the city as horizon for radical democracy. *ROAR Magazine*, 4 March.

Index